GATEWAY TO
CHINESE CLASSICAL LITERATURE

(Pre-Qin to Qing Dynasty)

Written by Li Xiaoxiang   Compiled by Asiapac Editorial
Illustrated by Fu Chunjiang   Translated by Yang Liping

℗ ASIAPAC • SINGAPORE

Publisher
ASIAPAC BOOKS PTE LTD
996 Bendemeer Road #06-09
Singapore 339944
Tel: (65) 6392 8455
Fax: (65) 6392 6455
Email: asiapacbooks@pacific.net.sg

Come visit us at our Internet home page
www.asiapacbooks.com

First published January 2005

Cover illustrations by Fu Chunjiang
Cover design by Koh Hong Teng
Body text in 11pt Times New Roman
Printed in Singapore by FuIsland Offset Printing (S) Pte Ltd

Publisher's Note

Literature is closely tied to the lives of people. In distant antiquity, to explain various natural phenomena, humans created grand and beautiful myths of creation; in work, recreation and religious rituals, poems and songs arose naturally to celebrate harvests, extol the joys of love and express respect for heaven and earth. When people began to consciously write to express their thoughts, it led to the flowering of literature and the contention of a hundred schools of thought.

With illustrations and lucid exposition of the various periods and styles of classical Chinese literature, we hope to provide valuable insights into the themes and social issues of early Chinese civilisation and inspire interest in Chinese literature at the same time.

We would like to thank Professor Li Xiaoxiang for the script, Mr Fu Chunjiang for his vibrant illustrations and Mr Yang Liping for the translation. Finally, we wish to thank the production team for making this publication possible.

Translator's Note

China boasts a spectacular civilisation in ancient times, especially during the Tang Dynasty. However, it went through a catastrophic attack and a tragic decline in a period from the late Qing Dynasty through the Republican Period (1911-1949) due to the combination of foreign infringements and domestic turmoil. Now, having recovered from the century-long nightmare, China is striding forward confidently and is believed by many to be growing rapidly into an economic, political and cultural power. In today's increasingly globalised world, China has become a country every nation has to reckon with.

Language study is not merely a linguistic matter because every language is deeply grounded in a given culture. Therefore, the best way for mastering a language such as Chinese is to develop your interest in the culture behind it, especially the literature written in that language which is undoubtedly a part and parcel of that culture. Here, Asiapac has contributed significantly by publishing this 'Gateway' book on the thousands years of classical Chinese literature. And I am also greatly honoured to have been entrusted by Asiapac with the task of translating the Chinese original script into English.

Yang Liping

About the Author

Professor Li Xiaoxiang, born in 1946, is currently the Deputy Editor-in-Chief of Wuhuan University Press.

Upon her graduation from Hunan Teachers' University, she has taught Chinese Language at pre-university level as well as worked in the Economic Department of the Zhejiang University's Higher Education Research Centre.

She has a deep understanding of Chinese language and literature. In particular, she is well-versed in Buddhism.

About the Illustrator

Fu Chunjiang, born in 1974, is a native of Chongqing municipality in southeastern China. A lover of traditional Chinese culture, he graduated in Chinese language studies.

He has been fond of drawing from childhood, and since 1994, he has been drawing comics. Among his works are *The Story of Kites* and *The Faint-Hearted Hero,* as well as the bestsellers *Origins of Chinese Festivals* and *Origins of Chinese People & Customs* published by Asiapac Books. He also participated in the production of *One Riddle for One Story*.

About the Translator

Yang Liping is currently a PhD candidate in the Department of English Language and Literature of the National University of Singapore, doing his research on the influence of translated foreign texts on the making of modern Chinese culture.

He taught English in a normal college in China for two years, obtained his MA from Shandong University (China) in 1995 and had worked as a full-time translator at Central Compilation and Translation Bureau (based in Beijing) for seven years.

His main interest is in literary translation and cultural exchange between China and the West in the pre-modern and modern periods. So far he has published over 10 book translations, including English-Chinese: *The British Museum Is Falling Down* (1998) and Chinese-English: *Old Cultural Works* (Cambridge Poetry Translation Series. Translated with Jeffrey Twitchell-Wass and Zheng Zhen, 2002).

Contents

Prologue

The literature of China can be traced back to the distant past. At that time, with only basic production tools and methods, people had to exert great effort in their work. As they laboured, they uttered rhythmic sounds such as "yo-ho, yo-ho" in time with their breaths. These rhythmic 'work songs' allowed them to coordinate their breathing and movements, reduce fatigue and increase productivity.

As these rhythmic work songs gradually grew richer in content, they evolved into metrical and meaningful poems. Later, people also liked to sing these songs and poems while dancing and offering sacrifices to gods or ancestors. Unfortunately, there was no written language during the prehistoric period and these early poems, which could only be handed down orally, are now lost to time.

The well-known 'Earth-Beating Song' below is said to have been handed down from the time of the legendary Emperors Yao and Shun.

We work at sunrise,
We rest at sunset.
Dig a well to drink,
Till the field to eat.
Of what avail are emperors to us?

PRE-QIN LITERATURE

Pre-Qin literature is the first chapter in the history of Chinese literature. Apart from the early ballads and myths, the literature of this period is represented mainly in poetry and prose. *The Book of Songs* and *Songs of the South* are two monuments in the history of ancient Chinese poetry. At the same time, historical and other types of prose writings of the Warring States Period are generally regarded as models of classical prose.

ANCIENT MYTHS

Myths were invented by ancient people to explain natural and cultural phenomena. For instance, when did the heaven and the earth come into being? Where did human beings come from? What are the sun, the moon, the stars, wind, rain, thunder and lightning? Lacking in scientific knowledge, the ancient people used their rich imagination to create many strange and fantastic stories and legends.

Before there was a written language, these myths were handed down orally. Later, some of them were recorded in the pre-Qin books and records. Of all pre-Qin books and records, *Classic of Mountains and Seas* is the richest source book of ancient myths, containing about 100 myths, which include familiar stories such as 'Nü Wa Patches the Sky', " Pan Gu separates Heaven from Earth, The Mythical Bird Jingwei Fills up the Sea' and 'Kuafu Chases the Sun'. These beautiful legends have had a far-reaching influence on later literature with the rich inspiration they offered.

Great Yu Controls the Floodwaters

Pan Gu Separates Heaven from Earth

Pre-Qin Mythology:

The Mythical Bird Jingwei Fills up the Sea

Nü Gua, the daughter of Emperor Yan, was playing at the beach of the East Sea.

How beautiful these shells are!

All of sudden, waves came up and took her away.

Help! Help!

Nü Gua changed into a little bird after her death.

You hideous sea, I swear to fill you up!

She tirelessly picked up branches and pebbles with her beak and threw them into the sea, though it was too deep and vast for her to fill.

People named the bird Jingwei. Its indomitable spirit epitomizes the early people's determination in their struggle against Nature.

THE BOOK OF SONGS

The Book of Songs, containing 305 poems, is the earliest anthology of poems extant in Chinese history and covers a period of about five centuries, extending from the early Western Zhou Dynasty (11th century BC) through the middle of the Spring and Autumn Period (6th century BC).

It is said that there were originally over 3,000 poems, but Confucius reduced the collection to the present number after careful selection. These poems were originally lyrics that were sung to melodies for rituals and ceremonies, and for entertainment as well. Later, the book became one of the five major Confucian classics (*Wu Jing*).

The book is divided into three parts —
Feng (Airs of the States), *Ya* (Elegantiae) and *Song* (Temple Hymns).
Feng collects folksongs from 15 regions. It is the largest part, comprising 160 folksongs, most of which reflect the lives and experiences of people.
Ya consists of songs performed in the imperial court of the Zhou Dynasty.
Song comprises songs chanted during sacrificial activities at ancestral temples.

Some of the finest verse in the book can be found in the poems of love.

Famous lines from *The Book of Songs*
Blue and blue is your collar, / Time and again I think of you. — 'Collar'
Dark green grow the rush leaves; / The white dewdrops turn to frost. / The woman whom I love, / Is on the opposite bank. — 'Rush Leaves'
My heart is down, / Who can understand? / Who can understand? — ' In the Garden Is a Peach-Tree'
Those who know me know I was sad at heart, / While those who did not know me wondered what I was seeking. — 'Millet Plump'
I will hold your hand, / And grow old with you. — 'Drumbeat'

Excerpt from *The Book of Songs*:

Chewk-chewk, an osprey whistles,
In the river from an isle.
Lo, a slim and graceful girl,
Fit for a man young and gentle.
Water mallow long and short grow,
Past her left and right flow.
Lo, a slim and graceful girl,
Pursue her awake or asleep.
Seek and court her yet in vain,
Still miss her awake or asleep.
There she is, but out of reach,
In bed I toss and turn, restless.

This poem describes a young man thinking of a girl. The bird's call makes him think about marrying her, using water mallow to express his sleepless longing and determined courtship.

Song Collectors

The Zhou government created a special official post to collect folksongs. Ringing a wooden bell, these officials visited various communities and recorded their lyrics.

The collectors handed the collected lyrics to court musicians. Once sorted and refined, the songs would then be presented to the emperor. These lyrics could help the emperor understand popular sentiments and social conditions.

Excerpt from *The Book of Songs*:

What grass does not wither?

What grass does not wither?
When do I not march?
What man is not forced
To go from here to there?
What grass does not blacken?
Who doesn't remain single?
A poor soldier am I,
Why not treat me as a human?
I am not a tiger or a bull,
Scampering in the wilderness.
A poor soldier am I,
Kept busy from dawn to dusk.

Wars broke out often during the Spring and Autumn and Warring States Periods. The ordinary folk saw their families torn apart, losing their homes and loved ones. Many young men were drafted to fight in the wars. This poem tells how soldiers were forced to rush here and there with little time for rest, living like wild beasts.

Artistic Features of *The Book of Songs*

Most of the poems in *The Book of Songs* have tetrasyllabic (four-character) lines. Sometimes phrases or lines of one stanza are repeated in another stanza with little or no change. This metrical recurrence is used to give the poem a musical effect. Common poetic techniques used include *Fu* (direct narration), *Bi* (figures of speech) and *Xing* (using what one sees in one's vision or mind's eye to introduce the theme).

QU YUAN — A GREAT PATRIOTIC POET

Qu Yuan (340–277 BC)

During the late Warring States Period, there appeared a new poetic form — *Chu Ci*, or *Songs of the South*. Based on folksongs in the southern state of Chu, they were revised by the patriotic poet Qu Yuan. The new form departed from the standard tetrasyllabic (four-character) lines set by *The Book of Songs*, with flexible syntax and many more lines. Written in ornate language, *Chu Ci* poems convey their meanings in an oblique way by drawing extensively on allusions to myths. Thus, they are filled with romantic flavour and charm. Another feature is that sound particles such as *xi* and *xie* are used quite often as caesuras.

Qu Yuan left behind 25 poems, including 'The Lament' (also known as 'On Encountering Sorrow'), 'Nine Songs', 'Nine Essays', 'Questioning Heaven', 'Distant Journey', 'Divination' and 'The Fisherman'. Depicting vividly the social conditions and political situation of the State of Chu and Qu Yuan's life of struggle, these poems are filled with deep concern about the country and the people, and showcase his dauntless spirit.

After Qu Yuan, the style continued to be adopted by men of letters such as Song Yu, Tang Le and Jing Chai. Song Yu stands out among them with his 'The Gaotang Rhapsody' and 'Rhapsody on the Holy Lady'. Liu Xiang of the Han Dynasty compiled the works of Qu Yuan and other writers of *Chu Ci* into an anthology under the title of *Chu Ci*, or *Songs of the South*. This is China's second poem anthology.

Footnote: *Li Sao: The Lament* published by Asiapac Books. ISBN 981-3029-22-6.

The Story of Qu Yuan

A noble of the State of Chu, Qu Yuan once served as a high-ranking official.

Later he lost favour with the King of Chu because of the slanders of venal officials at court.

He was demoted twice and exiled to the northern and western regions of the present Hunan province.

On hearing that the Qin army had conquered the Chu capital city of Ying, he was so overwhelmed by sorrow and anger that he took his life by throwing himself into the Miluo River.

His suicide occurred on the fifth day of the fifth lunar month. It was later set as a memorial date in his honour. On that day, people hold dragon-boat races and eat rice dumplings. So it is also called the Dragon-Boat Festival.

Excerpts from 'The Lament' by Qu Yuan:

'The Lament'

Qu Yuan's masterpiece, 'The Lament', contains 373 lines. It is regarded as the grandest lyrical poem in the history of ancient China. It is a personal statement by the poet, expressing his love for his country.

The road ahead is so long and so distant! I must travel up and down to seek my heart's desire.

In the poem, Qu Yuan pleaded with the King of Chu to reform the corrupt government and push the country back onto the right track, but the emperor would only listen to the slanderous talk of a group of sycophants. Feeling alone, Qu Yuan rode a whirlwind to the horizon, where an immortal advised him:

You'd better leave that dark place quickly to seek light and hope!

O! My hometown is in trouble. How can I bear to abandon it and go away!

Qu reached the land of light at last. But when he looked down, he caught sight of his troubled hometown, and could not bear to leave the country after all.

HISTORICAL WRITINGS

Courts of the Shang and Zhou Dynasties first established the position of historians. They recorded the emperors' words and deeds, and these records marked the beginnings of prose writing in China.

Shang Shu (*The Book of History*) is the earliest collection of prose writings in China. It covers the period from Emperor Yao's rule through the reign of King Mu of Qin.

Chun Qiu (*Spring and Autumn Annals*), reportedly compiled by Confucius, is a chronicle of the state of Lu. The author made criticisms in an understated style. This '*Chunqiu* style' had a lasting influence on later historical biographies.

Zuo Zhuan (*Zuo Commentary*) is a commentary on *Spring and Autumn Annals,* said to be written by Zuo Qiuming. The author drew on a great deal of historical data to interpret the subtleties in the *Annals* and delineate historical figures. The author's strength was in writing about war, and he discussed in detail the causes of wars and factors influencing their outcome.

Zhan Guo Ce (*Stratagems of the Warring States*) records the activities and speeches of political figures and strategists. Characters are vividly presented, the narrative is well-structured and dramatic, and it is also filled with allegories and metaphorical stories. Many familiar idioms used today are from this book, such as "*hu jia hu wei* (bully people by flaunting one's powerful connections)" and "*hua she tian zu* (add feet to a drawing of a snake)".

Pre-Qin Historical Writings:

Repulse the Qin Army with Quick Wits

from *Zuo Commentary*.

The Qin army was on its way to invade the State of Zheng. But the latter knew nothing about this.

A merchant from Zheng named Xuangao was travelling on business when he came across the Qin army.

Zheng is completely unprepared! What should I do?

Ah! I've got an idea!

Xuangao offered four tanned hides and twelve oxen to the Qin army as gifts.

Our king has heard that you are marching towards Zheng. He sent me to extend his best wishes.

Looks like the State of Zheng has made preparations. With no guarantee of victory, it's better for us to withdraw.

All right.

So Xuangao saved his country with his quick wits.

Adaptation from famous pre-Qin Historical Writings:

Su Dai Persuades King Hui of Zhao

from *Strategems of the Warring States*.

The State of Zhao was planning to invade the State of Yan. Su Dai came to dissuade King Hui of Zhao on behalf of Yan.

Your Majesty, as I passed the River Yi, I saw a clam on the bank…

The clam was basking in the warm sunshine with its shell open. A snipe came along then…

You will die if it doesn't rain today and tomorrow.

You won't survive either if I don't let go today and tomorrow!

Neither of them would give in. Finally, a fisherman came and caught them both.

Now Zhao is planning to invade Yan, but we won't give up easily. If the war drags on for a time, both sides will become weakened. I am afraid that it will be the State of Qin that benefits!

You're right. I've decided against invading Yan.

"When a snipe and a clam fight, the fisherman profits" later became an idiom.

PROSE WRITINGS OF
THE HUNDRED SCHOOLS

Many of the philosophical works of the pre-Qin period, such as *The Analects*, *Mencius*, *Xunzi*, *Laozi*, *Zhuangzi*, *Mozi* and *Hanfeizi*, written during the Spring and Autumn and Warring States Periods, have enduring literary value. Countless modern idiomatic expressions, such as "*wu shi bu xiao bai bu* (one who has retreated 50 steps laughing at another who has retreated 100 steps)" and "*jing di zhi wa* (a frog in the well)", have their origin in these works.

Laozi: The language is simple, yet profound. It uses vivid and sharp images to convey abstruse concepts.

Analects: A collection of the recorded words and deeds of Confucius. Written in the style of quotations, these records cannot be called prose writings in the truest sense.

Mencius: Full of vigour and passion, this work employs metaphors and argumentation to create a lively and vivid style.

Mozi: This work is written in plain and unadorned language. With its use of specific examples and rigorous logic, it broadened the range of philosophical writings.

Zhuangzi: Written in a literary style, this work contains a wealth of highly imaginative allegories, myths and stories.

Xunzi **and** ***Hanfeizi***: Works from the late Warring States Period. These works surpassed earlier prose writings in argumentation, reasoning and length.

Prose Writings of the Hundred Schools:

Fish and Bear's Paw

from *Mencius.*

I love fish, and I also love bear's paw.

If I cannot have both at the same time, I would give up fish and take bear's paw.

I cherish life, and I also uphold justice.

If I cannot have both at the same time, I would sacrifice life to uphold justice.

Prose Writings of the Hundred Schools:

Zhuangzi Dreams of a Butterfly

from *Zhuangzi*.

Zhuangzi had a dream. In the dream, he turned into a butterfly fluttering about with no cares.

Roaming through the natural world, the butterfly was very happy and forgot it was Zhuangzi.

Ah! I am still myself, not the butterfly.

Zhuangzi woke up from the dream.

Did I dream about turning into a butterfly? Or is the butterfly dreaming that it has turned into Zhuangzi?

Quotations from Prose Writings of the Hundred Schools

Isn't it a pleasant thing to study and review from time to time? Isn't it a pleasant thing to have friends coming from afar? — Analects of Confucius

If you know something and recognise that you know it; if you don't know something and realise that you don't know it. That is where knowledge arises. — Analects of Confucius

You can capture the commander of an army, but you cannot rid a common man of his will. — Analects of Confucius

The Way, if it can be articulated, is not the eternal Way. The name, if it can be named, is not the eternal name. — Laozi

Fortune may come of misfortune; and misfortune may be contained in fortune. — Laozi

True kindness is like water, which benefits all without competing. — Laozi

A true great man is someone whom money and rank cannot confuse, poverty and hardship cannot shake, and power and force cannot subjugate. — Mencius

Since you are not a fish, how can you know the happiness of being one? — Zhuangzi

All misfortunes, power struggles, grudges and hatred arise in the world when mutual love is nowhere to be found. — Mozi

The dye extracted from indigo is bluer than its source; just as ice is colder than water. — Xunzi

No awareness of evil exists where desire for profit prevails. — Hanfeizi

What is the Contention of a Hundred Schools?

The Spring and Autumn and Warring States Periods were a time of great turbulence in China. The country was fragmented into numerous small states which constantly attempted to annex one another through warfare. In the midst of these conflicts, everyone longed for the dawn of a new age.

During this time, a large number of thinkers emerged. They developed their own theories to explain the causes of social disorder and explore how to bring peace to the world. Major schools of thought included Confucianism (Confucius and Mencius), Taoism (Laozi and Zhuangzi), Legalism (Hanfeizi), Mohism (Mozi), etc.

LITERATURE OF THE HAN DYNASTY

In 221 BC, China was unified under the Qin Dynasty. Emperor Qin Shihuang burnt books and buried Confucian scholars alive, causing havoc to the Chinese culture. However, Qin also unified the Chinese script, thus making a great contribution to the development of Chinese literature. However, the Qin Dynasty lasted only 15 years (221–206 BC) and left no important literary works. The Han dynasty was founded in 206 BC, and ushered in a Golden Age for the Chinese nation. Consisting of two periods — the Western Han (206 BC–AD 25) and the Eastern Han (AD 25–220), the Han Dynasty saw literature separating from scholarship and moving towards independence.

POEMS OF MONARCHS

Two of the most famous poems from the dawn of the Han Dynasty are Xiang Yu's 'Song at Gaixia' and Liu Bang's 'Ode to the Gale'.

Xiang Yu (232–202 BC)

Xiang Yu was Liu Bang's foremost rival in the struggle to gain control of the country. Xiang Yu's forces were stronger, but he was defeated in the end. In 202 BC., Xiang Yu was surrounded by Liu's army at Gaixia. At the end of his rope, he wrote a sad song to his beloved concubine Lady Yu. 'Song at Gaixia' evokes the despair of a hero who has failed, yet remains brave and heroic.

Once unrivalled in strength,
I could pluck up the hill.
But now I'm forsaken by the times,
And my steed runs no more.
When it cannot run
What then can I do?
Oh, Yu, my dear Yu,
How shall I help you next?"

Liu Bang (247–95 BC)

The first time Liu Bang returned to his hometown after founding the Han Dynasty and becoming emperor, he invited his townsmen to a feast. Enjoying the wine very much, Liu composed an ode while playing the *zhu* (an ancient stringed instrument). 'Ode to the Gale' contains only 23 characters, but it is filled wtih lofty sentiments.

"O! The gale is rising,
And clouds scudding.
My might has spread across the four seas,
And now I am back at my old village.
How shall I get warriors
To guard the four corners of my land? "

HAN *FU* (RHYMED PROSE POETRY)

After the founding of the Han Dynasty, *Chu Ci*, or *Songs of the South*, which was established by Qu Yuan, became the dominant literary form. Later, another form of rhymed prose poetry based on the ornate and extravagant style of *Chu Ci* was developed, called Han *Fu*. Among the major Han *Fu* writers are Jia Yi, Mei Cheng and Sima Xiangru.

Jia Yi (200–168 BC)

Jia Yi was an honest official in the Han court. He was banished because of slanders against him. One day, a large owl flew into his room. The owl was considered an ill omen, and this led him to think of his own frustrated situation He composed 'Rhapsody on an Owl'. In the poem, he makes use of an imaginary dialogue with the bird to comfort himself.

Mei Cheng (Unknown–140 BC)

Mei Cheng is known for 'The Seven Stimuli'. In this work, the crown prince of the State of Chu is ill and a courtier from the State of Wu tries to provoke him by telling him seven things. On hearing them, the prince breaks into a sweat and makes an immediate recovery. The work is grand in scope and vivid in description.

Sima Xiangru (ca. 179–118 BC)

One of the most important *Fu* writers, Sima Xiangru is also well-known for his having eloped with Zhuo Wenjun. During the reign of Emperor Wu of the Han Dynasty, Empress Ah Jiao fell into disfavor and was relegated to limbo. She asked Sima Xiangru to write 'Changmen Rhapsody' for her; and presented it to the emperor. Reading it, the emperor was deeply moved. Other famous works by Sima Xiangru are 'Rhapsody on Mr Void' and 'Rhapsody on the Imperial Garden of Shanglin'.

Sima Xiangru and Zhuo Wenjun

Though he was a talented man, Sima Xiangru was very poor. Once he played the zither at a banquet given by Zhuo Wangsun, the wealthiest man in Linqiong.

Bravo! What a talented man!

Zhuo Wangsun's daughter was a talented woman. Unfortunately, she was widowed at a young age, and lived in her parents' home.

Sima Xiangru had also admired Zhuo Wenjun for a long time. So he proposed to her through her maidservant.

My father won't agree. But to be with Sima Xiangru, I won't care about my name!

So Zhuo Wenjun left her home that very evening and eloped with Sima to his old hometown.

Wenjun, I'm sorry that you'll have to lead a poor life with me.

As long as I can be with a confidant like you, poverty means nothing to me.

Later, the couple came back to Linqiong and opened a small wine shop. Zhuo Wenjun sold wines while Sima Xiangru served tables and washed dishes.

That is Zhuo Wangsun's daughter!

The waiter is the talented Sima Xiangru!

Feeling shamed, Zhuo Wangsun gave Zhuo Wenjun some money to make sure that the couple could get by. So the wine shop was closed.

Later, Sima Xiangru gained the favour of Emperor Wu, who sent him on a diplomatic mission to southwest China. When he stopped by Linqiong, the local gentry welcomed him with fine wines.

It is said that, after becoming rich and noble, Sima Xiangru wanted to take a young and pretty concubine. At this, Zhuo Wenjun wrote a poem titled 'Song of White Hair' for him.

Hearing your love is divided, I have come to bid adieu... marriage should not bring so many tears... I wished for a man of true heart, that we would not part though our hairs turn white...

My daughter has made a good choice!

Wenjun has been through so much with me. How can I let her down! I won't take a concubine.

23

YUEFU SONGS
(BUREAU OF MUSIC)

Folksongs reached a peak during the Han Dynasty. These songs were collected and revised by the official Bureau of Music (*Yuefu*) into poems and set to music to perform during court ceremonies and banquets. Hence they were often called *Yuefu* songs. Some poets also modelled their works on the style of such songs. Historical records show that 138 *yuefu* songs were collected during the Western Han Dynasty. But today, many of them have been lost and there are just over 40 extant. Mainly narrative, these poems are written in various forms, such as tetrasyllabic (four-character) lines, pentasyllabic (five-character) lines and mixed ones (the number of characters per line is not fixed throughout a poem), but exhibit a tendency towards the more regular pentasyllabic style.

A famous *Yuefu* folksong

A Peacock Flying to the Southeast
Containing more than 1,700 characters, it is the longest ancient Chinese poem.
It tells of a young couple, Liu Lanzhi and her husband Jiao Zhongqing. Jiao Zhongqing's mother disliked her and they had to separate. They agreed to find a way to reunite someday.
However, when Liu Lanzhi returned home, her elder brother forced her to marry the son of the local prefect. Learning of this, Jiao Zhongqing

believed that she had betrayed him. To prove her love, she committed suicide by throwing herself into a pond. Jiao Zhongqing hanged himself soon after her death. Filled with remorse, the two families agreed to bury the couple together and planted pine and phoenix trees by their tomb.

Branches were woven together, and leaf entwined about leaf; Within them dwelt a pair of birds, styling themselves mandarin ducks. Heads raised, they sang to each other, until the hour of dawn every night.

NINETEEN ANCIENT POEMS

The authorship of the *Nineteen Ancient Poems* is unknown. They are short pentasyllabic poems, concerned with social conditions and human emotions, especially love. Though written in simple and colloquial language, these nineteen poems are evocative and lyrical, marking the maturity of this poetic form.

Selections from *Nineteen Ancient Poems*

The Cowherd Star Far and Away

The cowherd star is far and away,
The star of weaving girl clear and bright.
Slim white hands working nonstop
On the loom down and up.
She has not finished the cloth today;
Her tears roll down like rain.
The Milky Way is clear and shallow,
When will they meet again?
Separated by a torrential river,
She can only gaze lovingly.

Drawing on the popular folktale of the cowherd and the weaving girl, this poem uses the weaving girl's longing for the cowherd to express the sorrow of a wife unable to be with her husband.

Walk and Stop, Stop and Walk (excerpt)

Walk and stop, stop and walk.
From you I am separated.
Ten thousand miles between us,
You and I at two ends of heaven.
The road ahead is rough and long,
Who knows when we will meet again?
Along the north wind Tartar horses run,
On southern boughs southern birds nest.

This poem describes a girl whose lover is away on a journey and tells how difficult it is for them to be parted by great distances and unable to meet.

RECORDS OF THE GRAND HISTORIAN

Historical Masterpiece — *Records of the Grand Historian*
Records of the Grand Historian written by Sima Qian's (145–90 BC) during the Western Han dynasty represents the pinnacle of historical prose writings in China. As the first comprehensive historical work in China, it records political, economic, cultural and artistic history spanning a period of three thousand years from the time of legendary Yellow Emperor (Huangdi) to the reign of Emperor Wu of the Han Dynasty.

Containing 130 essays, the work is divided into sections such as Biographies (biographies of dynastic rulers), Houses (chronicling old and well-known families) and Traditions (dealing with the common people).Unraveling the complicated historical events around biographies of individual characters, it presents a series of vivid vignettes of emperors, ministers, generals, strategists, knights-errant, poets, scholars, ordinary people and even criminals.

Records of the Grand Historian featuress dramatic storylines, succinct and vivid language, and frequent use of proverbs and common sayings. Lu Xun, a great writer of modern China, regarded the book highly, praising it as "the acme of historical writings, an unrhymed 'The Lament' (a poem by Qu Yuan)."

Quotations from *Records of the Grand Historian*

For a hero, nothing can make him cower! — Biography of Emperor Gaozu

Books will only let me know my name. A sword only deals with one adversary — it is not worth learning. I will learn to defeat ten thousand men. — Biography of Xiang Yu

Lo, what does a sparrow know of a swan's lofty ambitions? — House of Chen She

O the wind is blowing hard along the cold Yi River; the departing hero will not return alive. — Traditions of Assassins

Like a rat, whether a man is good depends where he abides. — Traditions of Li Si

The Story of Sima Qian

Sima Qian was already very knowledgeable at an early age, having read nearly all the books by the Hundred Schools and travelled widely.

His father served as Prefect Grand Historian under Emperor Wu. He passed away when Sima Qian was 36, and Sima Qian inherited his father's official title.

Later, Sima Qian angered Emperor Wu when he pleaded the case of General Li Ling, who had surrendered to the Huns.

The Emperor sentenced him to castration as punishment.

Fired by this humiliation, Sima Qian became even more determined and hard-working. He spent 18 years writing the *Records of the Grand Historian*.

Excerpt from the *Records of the Grand Historian*

A Banquet at Hongmen

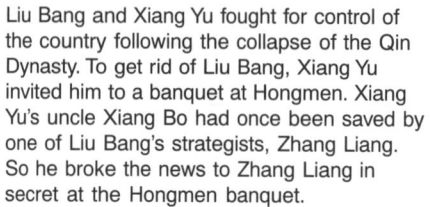

Liu Bang and Xiang Yu fought for control of the country following the collapse of the Qin Dynasty. To get rid of Liu Bang, Xiang Yu invited him to a banquet at Hongmen. Xiang Yu's uncle Xiang Bo had once been saved by one of Liu Bang's strategists, Zhang Liang. So he broke the news to Zhang Liang in secret at the Hongmen banquet.

Come on! Cheers! Let's have a good drink!

Grand General, I have taken control of Xianyang. I will obey whatever order you issue.

Your Majesty, we should not hesitate to get rid of Liu Bang.

Liu Bang is only a nobody. He is also very polite and respectful to me. If I kill him. all people would pour ridicule on me.

So, Fan Zeng gave Xiang Yu's cousin Xiang Zhuang stealthy instructions.

You can perform swordplay to liven up the banquet and seek a chance to kill Liu Bang.

Seeing this, Xiang Bo also pulled out his sword and joined in the performance to protect Liu Bang. Xiang Zhuang did not get a chance to assassinate Liu Bang.

Liu Bang's bodyguard Fan Kuai walked into the tent, holding a sword and a shield in hand.

Who are you?

He is Liu Bang's bodyguard Fan Kuai.

What a hero he is! Give him a cup of wine and a leg of pork!

Fan Kuai downed the wine and placed the leg of pork on his shield, cutting it into big pieces to eat.

Very good! Hero, can you drink more?

I am not afraid of death. Drinking wine is nothing at all!

The emperor of Qin was a despot, so everybody rose up against him. Lord Liu has defeated the Qin army, yet you want to kill him, following in the footsteps of a despot.

... ...

Afterwards, Liu Bang excused himself by saying that he wanted to go to the toilet and left without saying goodbye.

Sigh! The one who will conquer the country is surely Lord Liu!

HISTORY OF THE WESTERN HAN DYNASTY

The First Book of Dynastic History

Another outstanding work on history, the *History of the Western Han Dynasty*, was written by Ban Gu (AD 32–92) during the Eastern Han Dynasty. It is the first book of dynastic history (recording only the Western Han dynasty) in China. Also a noted *fu* writer, Ban Gu used many elegant yet moderate parallelisms and couplets in the book, which exerted some influence on later historiographers.

A Family Devoted to Historiography

Ban Gu's father Ban Biao was also a historian. He wrote 65 historical accounts on the history of the Western Han Dynasty in a style modeled on *Records of the Grand Historian*. He also compiled these accounts into a book called *A Supplement to Records of the Grand Historian*.

After his father passed away, Ban Gu carried on the family tradition and decided to write a great historical book like *Records of the Grand Historian*. This was usually the work of court-appointed historians. Ban Gu's personal effort was considered a crime and resulted in his arrest. Later, Emperor Ming read his manuscript and was pleased. Ban Gu was set free and allowed to continue writing the *History of the Western Han Dynasty*. It took him over 20 years to finish the book. Later, he was embroiled in another court case and died in prison. As a small part (eight tables and astronomical records) of the book had not been completed, Emperor He decreed that Ban Gu's sister Ban Zhao should take over. Thus, the book was finally completed. Ban Zhao is also a distinguished woman writer in Chinese history.

Literature of Wei, Jin, Southern and Northern Dynasties

The Wei, Jin, Southern and Northern Dynasties were a time of severe social instability and political corruption. However, it was also a time of growing self-awareness for Chinese literature. The literati pursued mental and spiritual freedom and took delight in mountains and rivers, and the pastoral life. This ushered in the rise of pastoral poetry, of which Tao Yuanming is an outstanding representative, exerting a far-reaching influence on the later literature.

JIAN'AN LITERATURE

In AD 196, Cao Cao relocated the imperial capital to Xuchang on the order of Emperor Xian. The emperor's reign title was changed to Jian'an; hence literary works of this period and some time after are incorporated under a general term — Jian'an literature. In this chaotic time, many poets addressed topics such as current affairs and broken families, voicing their sentiments and ideals. This lent a heroic yet sorrowful tone to the literature of this period.

Representative poets of this period include Cao Cao and his two sons — Cao Pi and Cao Zhi, known jointly as "the Three Caos"; and the Seven Masters of the Jian'an Era (Kong Rong, Chen Lin, Wang Can, Xu Xi, Ruan Yu, Ying Chang and Liu Zhen).

Cao Cao (AD 155–220)
Cao Cao is both the foremost statesman and the centre of the literary scene at that time. Impassioned and forceful, Cao Cao's poetry expresses his great ambitions and an intense sorrow over the fast passage of time.

Cao Pi (AD 187–226)
The second son of Cao Cao, Cao Pi later ascended the throne of the Kingdom of Wei. His *On Literature* is China's first literary monograph, paving the way for Chinese literary criticism.

Cao Zhi (AD 192–232)
He is the third and also the most talented son of Cao Cao. However, his brother Cao Pi was suspicious of him and he was nearly killed by Cao Pi. A popular legend tells how he composed a poem within seven paces. His best known work is 'The Goddess of the River Luo'.

Selected poems by Cao Cao:

A Short Song (excerpt)
Singing to the wine I wonder:
How long shall a man live?
Like the morning dew,
Painfully fast time flies.
Feeling sad and vehement,
I'm wrapped by pensive thoughts.
What can dispel my anxiety?
Only Du Kang (wine).

Though the Tortoise Is Blessed with A Life Long (excerpt)
An old steed is stabled,
Yet it longs to gallop a thousand miles.
An ambitious man, advanced in years,
Never abandons his proud aspirations.

Cao Zhi Composes a Poem in Seven Paces

SEVEN SAGES OF THE BAMBOO GROVE

After the death of Cao Pi, Cao Rui ascended the throne. When Cao Rui died, Cao Fang succeeded him. The young Cao Fang had to seek the help of Cao Shuang and Sima Yi in running the government. In AD 249, Sima Yi launched a coup d'état and eliminated Cao Shuang. From then onwards, Cao Fang was merely a nominal emperor, with true power in the hands of the Sima family.

Though displeased with the high-handed Sima family, many scholars knew that it was very dangerous to oppose them. Therefore, some talented figures sought escape by indulging in wine and poems while others chose to lead a bohemian and eccentric life.

Among these individuals, the most important are Ruan Ji, Ji Kang, Shan Tao, Wang Rong, Xiang Xiu, Liu Ling and Ruan Xian, known collectively as the Seven Sages of the Bamboo Grove. They wrote poems and essays to express their dissatisfaction and resentment.

Ruan Ji (AD 210–263)

Among the Seven Sages, Ruan Ji was the most accomplished, but because of the corruption and power struggles in the court, he decided to distance himself from worldly affairs. He enjoyed drinking and was often drunk, but it was also a way of avoiding trouble.

Poem from the Heart by Ruan Ji

Being sleepless late at night,
I rise to pluck the zither.
On the thin curtain shines the bright moon,
A cool breeze sways the front of my gown.
A lone swan moans in the wilderness,
Flying birds chitter in the northern groves.
Pacing up and down, unsure what to see,
Mournful thoughts rise and press my heart.

This is one of the 82 poems written by the poet with the same title, 'Poem from the Heart', reflecting obliquely the dark side of social reality and the poet's dejected feelings.

Ruan Ji Rolls Up His Eyes

Ruan Ji's mother had passed away. Ji Kang's brother Ji Xi visited him to offer his condolences.

Ji Xi was an official caught up in seeking fame and profit. Ruan Ji did not like him and rolled up his eyes when he greeted Ji Xi.

When Ji Kang came over with zither and wine, Ruan Ji welcomed him warmly.

Drinking and enjoying Ji Kang's music, Ruan Ji beamed with an attentive look.

In ancient times, drinking and entertainment were deemed improper during mourning. Ruan Ji and Ji Kang did this as a way to revolt against these restrictive rules.

Ji Kang (AD 223–262)

A relative of the royal family of the Kingdom of Wei, Ji Kang was a close friend of Ruan Ji. He was a highly accomplished man of letters deeply influenced by Lao Zi and Zhuang Zi. Indifferent to fame and gains, he preferred to stay at home reading poems and playing the zither. It is reported that he was taught by a mysterious man to play the famous 'Melody of Guangling'.

Ji Kang as a Blacksmith

In his free time, Ji Kang liked to work at his forge beneath a willow tree outside his house.

A young nobleman, Zhong Hui, came to see him because of his fame. Ji Kang ignored him and continued working.

Angered at being snubbed, Zhong Hui turned to leave.

Hearing what I heard, I came, and having seen what I have seen, I now depart.

What did you hear that made you come, and what have you seen that now makes you leave?

Zhong Hui harboured a grudge against Ji Kang and later framed him. Ji Kang was executed on the orders of Sima Zhao. Before the execution, Ji Kang was allowed to play 'The Melody of Guangling'. This famous song was lost forever with his death.

PASTORAL POET — TAO YUANMING

Tao Yuanming (AD 365–427)

After the fall of the Kingdom of Wei, the Jin Dynasty was founded. The Jin Dynasty falls into two stages — the Western Jin and the Eastern Jin. Among the great writers who emerged during the Eastern Jin is Tao Yuanming.

He was unaffected in mannerisms and loved nature, and these qualities are clearly reflected in his poetry.

His style is elegant and unadorned, expressing his carefree and imperturbable state of mind. Before Tao Yuanming, pastoral imagery such as dogs, chickens and mulberry trees was rare, but through his pen, these subjects become fresh and filled with interest. Many later writers such as Li Bai, Bai Juyi, Wang Wei and Su Shi were all lavish in their praise of Tao Yuanming's works.

A Famous Poem by Tao Yuanming

Drinking Wine: No. 5

I made my home where people reside,
Yet hear no clamour of horse or cart.
How, you ask, can this be so?
A distant heart makes the place remote.
Plucking chrysanthemums by the east fence,
I leisurely look to the southern hills.
The mountain air is more agreeable at dusk,
Birds fly home to roost together.
A deeper meaning lies in this;
I try to explain and forget the words.

This poem describes the carefree bucolic life, and is one of the most representative of Tao Yuanming's poetry.

I won't bend my back for five *dou* of rice

Tao Yuanming was born into a family of officials. His father died when he was 12 and his family came down in the world. After he grew up, he did not want an official post, preferring to stay at home to read, farm and take care of his aged mother.

Later, when it became harder to make ends meet, he was forced to take an official post. However, he felt rather stifled by the life of an official.

This isn't the right place for me!

When Tao was working as a magistrate in Pengze County, an inspector sent by the prefect came for an inspection .

Huh! This man always oppresses the people.

Should I dress up and welcome such a flunkey? No, I would rather give up my salary of five *dou** of rice than bend my back before him!

So, Tao Yuanming surrendered his official seal and resigned.

From then on, Tao Yuanming retired to the countryside he loved, working for himself, relating well to the farmers and composing many beautiful pastoral poems.

* *An ancient Chinese unit of measure.*

A Story of the Peach Blossom Spring

This is the most famous prose work by Tao Yuanming and it expresses the longing of people for a pure and carefree place like the Peach Blossom Spring.

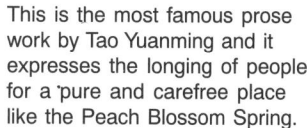

There was a fisherman in Wuling during the Jin Dynasty. One day he went into a forest of peach trees by boat.

Oh, no! I seem to have lost my way.

Then, he entered an opening in the mountains and found a small village.

The village had fertile fields and the peoke all looked happy and carefree.

Where am I now on earth?

Our forefathers lived during the Qin Dynasty.

To escape the wars and chaos, they found this place hidden from the world. Many generations have passed and we have never gone out.

When the fisherman left, he took care to mark his route.

When I come again, I can find the way.

Later, when he attempted to return, he could not find the way again.

LANDSCAPE POETS —
XIE SENIOR AND JUNIOR

The Southern Dynasties witnessed the flowering of landscape poetry, a genre that focuses on mountain-and-river landscapes as subjects. Metaphysical poetry, which had dominated the poetic scene for a time, was becoming increasingly hollow and dull. Poets began to turn their focus from metaphysical contemplation while enjoying scenery to appreciation of the landscape itself, hence the rise of landscape poetry. Xie Lingyun and Xie Tiao are two prominent landscape poets of the Southern Dynasties and are known as "Xie Senior and Junior".

Xie Lingyun (AD 385–433)

Xie Lingyun is the first poet to concentrate on writing landscape poetry. Born into a rich and powerful family during the Eastern Jin Dynasty, he was given the title of Duke Kangle at the age of 18. Later, political setbacks caused him to turn his attention to natural beauty, which he depicted in his verse in an elegant and refined style, stimulating the development of the genre.

Xie Tiao (AD 464–499)

Xiao Tiao's landscape poetry is fresh and natural in style. He often used his poems to express a sense of frustration with life. With his close attention to rhyme, meter and other technical aspects, his verse is smooth and easy to read. His poetry was so popular that that there was a saying, "You will feel as if you have bad breath if you don't read Xie Tiao's poems for three days."

A Landscape Poem by Xie Tiao

From Xinlinpu through Xuancheng towards Banqiao
The river's path extends far into the southwest,
Comes rushing back towards the northeast.
At the horizon is seen a returning boat,
Amidst the clouds, river trees are spotted.

FOLKSONGS OF THE SOUTHERN AND NORTHERN DYNASTIES

During the Southern and Northern Dynasties, China remained divided between the south and the north for a long time. The two regions had distinct environments, social customs and ethnic compositions, and these cultural differences were reflected in their folksongs as well. The southern folksongs deal mainly with the amorous feelings between men and women, whereas the northern folksongs are forthright and have a wide range of subject matters. Besides love, northern folksongs also describe the brutality of war, arduous living experiences and local scenery. Well-known folksongs include 'The Ballad of Mulan', about Hua Mulan, who disguised herself as a man to serve in the army in her father's place, and 'Song of Chile', which limns the beauty of the vast northern steppes.

Selected Folksongs of the Southern and Northern Dynasties

A Ziye Song (from the Southern Dynasties)
The first time you caught my eye,
I hoped our hearts could be as one.
Now, feeding the silk into a broken loom,
Surely not a bolt of cloth can be made.

Song of Chile (from the Northern Dynasties)
Chile River,
Runs below the Yin Mountain.
The sky looks like a yurt,
Enveloping the wilderness.
The sky so hazy,
The wilderness so vast,
And the wind, bending the grass, reveals flocks and herds.

CLASSICAL CHINESE SHORT STORIES

During the Wei, Jin, Southern and Northern Dynasties, the two main types of short stories featured tales of the supernatural and anecdotes of personalities.

Stories of Immortals and Ghosts

Buddhism and Taoism were very popular during this turbulent time, leading to stories of the supernatural. Better-known works include Gan Bao's *In Search of Spirits* and Liu Yiqing's *Collection of Ghost Stories*. Despite the supernatural themes, these stories express public sentiments and reveal the darkness in society.

Liu and Ruan Enter Tiantai Mountain

from *In Search of Spirits*.

During the Eastern Han Dynasty, Liu Chen and Ruan Zhao lost their way in the mountain one day.

They ran into two pretty girls who invited them to their home as guests.

Ten days later.

We are very homesick and would like to take our leave now.

When they returned to their village…

Why can't we recognise anyone?

It isn't the Han Dynasty any more. It's the Jin Dynasty.

Stories about Personalities

Stories of this type are the result of the trend of "pure conversations" that prevailed during this period. The words, deeds and morals of men of letters became the focus of attention and commentary after the close of the Wei-Jin period, and this directly ushered in the genre of stories about personalities. The best-known stories of this type are collected in *A New Account of Tales of the World*. They are very short and similar in form to modern short stories.

Freedom and Restraint

from *A New Account of Tales of the World.*

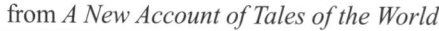

Wang Huizhi was drinking wine and enjoying the snowy night.	I must go to see Dai Andao while I am in such high spirits.	He headed for Dai's residence in a boat that very night.
Standing there for a while, he did not knock the door.	Then he went back on the boat.	Why did you turn back without knocking? / I came in high spirits. But the mood is gone, so what's the point of seeing him?

The Trend of "Pure Conversations" during the Wei and Jin Dynasties

During the Wei, Jin, Southern and Northern Dynasties people liked to gather together in forests or bamboo groves to engage in rambling talks. To demonstrate their upright and outstanding moral qualities, they never talked about social and political affairs. Rather they devoted themselves to empty talks on metaphysical ideas. This is the so-called trend of "pure conversations".

PARALLEL PROSE

Parallel prose refers to a prose style characterized by regular symmetrical four-character or six-character lines. Ornate and metrical in language, parallel prose is also packed with literary allusions.

Chinese literature entered a stage of self-consciousness following the Wei-Jin period. Men of letters began to pursue beauty in symmetry and place increasing emphasis on the art of parallelism. This tendency reached a peak during the Qi and Liang Dynasties.

However, the overemphasis on beauty in form also prevented writers from expressing their thoughts and feelings freely. Some men of letters had already criticised this prose style during the Six Dynasties. During the Tang and Song Dynasties, there was even a campaign to reform the prose style and advocating the abandonment of parallel prose.

Literary Criticism

Two critical monographs appeared during the period:
- Liu Xie's *The Literary Mind and the Carving of Dragons* is a compendium of literary theory and criticism, considerably influencing later literary criticism.
- Zhong Rong's *The Grades of Poetry* is the earliest monograph on poetic criticism.

LITERATURE OF THE TANG DYNASTY

Chinese literature flourished during the Tang Dynasty, particularly poetry, which arguably embodies the spirit of the age. Among the numerous poets active in this lively literary atmosphere are such great names as Li Bai, Du Fu and Bai Juyi, who left us many vibrant, immortal works. Tang poetry can be divided into four periods — Early Tang, High Tang, Mid-Tang and Late Tang.

FOUR ELITES OF EARLY TANG

The Four Elites of Early Tang refer to four talented poets: Lu Zhaolin, Luo Binwang, Wang Bo and Yang Jiong. Among them Luo Binwang and Wang Bo are better-known.

Luo Binwang (AD 619–687)

Luo Binwang was considered a child prodigy because of the extraordinary talent he displayed in childhood. Later, he gained the favor of Emperor Gaozong and was granted an official post, but was imprisoned because he offended Empress Wu Zetian. When he was released, he joined in a movement against Wu Zetian. He drafted an official denunciation of Wu Zetian, detailing her crimes in sharp and strong terms. When Wu Zetian read the document, she was not angry at all and even admired his talent greatly.

Ode to the Goose

Goose, goose, goose,
Bending your neck skywards you sing.
White feathers floating on green water,
Red feet pushing the clear waves.

This is a poem composed by Luo Binwang when he was seven. One day, he was walking with his father and a guest by the pond when a gaggle of geese swam past. The guest asked him to compose a poem about the waterfowl. So he came up with the above poem extempore.

Wang Bo (AD 650–676)

A quick-witted man of letters, Wang Bo could write an essay as quick as thought. A legend goes that whenever he wanted to write, he would prepare a bowl of Chinese ink and drink it in one gulp before going to bed. As soon as he woke up, he would put brush to paper and write out an essay very quickly. Therefore, it is often said that he composed a draft in his stomach before writing out the essay. Wang Bo led a short and troubled life. He was drowned at sea at the age of 27.

Seeing Vice-Magistrate Du off to His Post in Sichuan

By the wall around the three Qin districts, mists making five rivers one,
I bid you farewell, both officials travelling.
While there is friendship within the four seas,
Thousands of miles are but a stone's throw.
At the place of separation, please don't
Wipe your eyes like a heartbroken child.

This is a poem that Wang Bo wrote when seeing off a friend, and it demonstrates the optimistic, carefree and forward-thinking mindset of the poet. The lines "While there is friendship within the four seas, Thousands of miles are but a stone's throw" have been passed down through the years.

Wang Bo's
'Preface to Tengwang Pavilion'

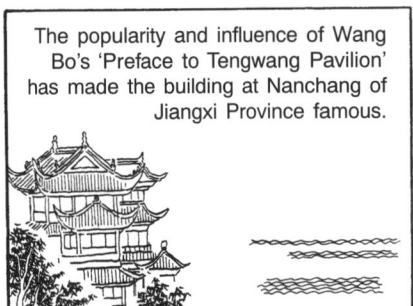

The popularity and influence of Wang Bo's 'Preface to Tengwang Pavilion' has made the building at Nanchang of Jiangxi Province famous.

During the Double Ninth Festival*, Prefect Yan Boyu of Nanchang held a banquet at Tengwang Pavilion. He asked his son-in-law to write an essay to commemorate the event in advance.

You can show it off during the banquet.

At the banquet...

Today is the Chong Yang Festival. You're all noted men of letters. I hope sincerely that you can write some rhymed prose to mark this occasion.

We have only poor talents and learning; we won't show ourselves up.

The guests already knew about Prefect Yan's plan...

I am Wang Bo. Allow me to write a piece.

I must attend to something. Please go on.

Yan Boyu was angered and excused himself.

He instructed servants to report to him what Wang Bo had written.

Lord, he has just written, "the evening glow drifts with a lone mallard; the hue of the autumn river mingles with the vast sky."

What a genius!

This is how Wang Bo's famed 'Preface to Tengwang Pavilion' came about. Knowing that the piece by his son-in-law was inferior, Yan Boyu did not produce it.

*Also known as the Chong Yang Festival.

Chen Zi'ang (AD 661–702)

Another great poet of the early Tang is Chen Zi'ang. He was an advocate of innovation in poetry and prose, proposing that the ornate poetic style of the Southern dynasties should be swept away and wholesome contents be injected into poetry. Born into a wealthy family, Chen Zi'ang passed the highest-level Imperial Civil Service Examination at the age of 24, but subsequent setbacks undermined his political ambitions.

On Climbing Youzhou Tower
Where have all the ancient sages gone?
And where are the coming generations?
Thinking of heaven and earth broad and vast,
I plunge into sorrow with my tears streaming down.

Chen Zi'ang and the *Hu* Lute

When Chen Zi'ang was 21, he travelled to Luoyang.

No one knows me. I need to think of a way to gain notice.

Hu lute, one million coppers each.

So expensive!

I'll take it.

Everybody, come to my place tomorrow. I will play a tune for you.

The following day, he broke the precious lute.

Playing the lute is nothing. These poems are much better.

Thus, Chen Zi'ang's fame spread, and after they read his poems, his talent was soon widely acknowledged.

THE HIGH TANG CLIMATE

The reign of Emperor Xuanzong, which is divided into Kaiyuan and Tianbao periods, is referred to as the High Tang period. During this time, the economy and cultural achievements of the Tang Dynasty was at their peak. Though it lasted only 43 years (713–755), it was a golden age for Chinese poetry, which developed at an unprecedented pace. Poems written during this period are rich in content and vigorous in style. The term, "High Tang climate", is often used to describe the vibrancy and spirit of poetic works of this period.

Many outstanding poets appeared during this period. The first wave comprised poets like Zhang Jiuling, He Zhizhang and Zhang Ruoxu. However, later poets such as Wang Wei, Meng Haoran, Gao Shi, Cen Can, Wang Changling, Li Bai and Du Fu are more representative of this period. Wang Wei and Meng Haoran represented pastoral poetry while Gao Shi, Cen Can and Wang Changling headed the school of frontier poetry. Li Bai is known as the Poetry Deity, while Du Fu is called the Sage of Poetry.

He Zhizhang (AD 659–744)
Bold and unconstrained in nature, He Zhizhang loved drinking and was known as one of the "Eight Drunken Immortals," which include Li Bai and Zhang Xu. It is said that he would write wonderful poems and essays whenever he was drunk, but could not do so once he sobered up. He was also a distinguished calligrapher and whenever he was drunk and in high spirits, people would prepare brush and paper and invite him to write something.

Coming Home
I left home young and return old,
My accents remain but my hair gray.
The children I meet do not know me,
Smiling, they ask from whence I come.

This poem, easily understood and flowing smoothly off the tongue, vividly illustrates a traveller's emotions on returning home.

Meng Haoran (AD 689–740)

Meng Haoran is the first poet in the Tang Dynasty devoted to writing bucolic poetry. His poetry is natural, smooth and fresh and is praised as "clear poetry." He had never taken an official post and led a life of travelling and seclusion.

Spring Dawn

Springtime sleeper unaware of dawn,
All around the chittering of birds.
Sounds of rain and wind at night,
How many blossoms have fallen?

This poem reflects the idyllic and carefree life of the poet. The language is clear and simple, smooth and flowing.

Wang Zhihuan (AD 688–742)

No information is available in historical records about Wang Zhihuan's life. He left behind only six poems, among which two have earned him a lasting reputation — 'Climbing the Heron Pavilion' and the frontier poem, 'A Song of Liangzhou'.

Climbing the Heron Pavilion

The bright sun shines beyond the ridges,
The Yellow River flowing to the sea.
If you would behold a grander sight
You will have to climb up one more storey.

The first two lines of this simple poem sum up the sights from the Heron Pavilion, while the last two lines are thought-provoking. Only when you stand at a higher place can you see farther. If you want to make greater progress, you will have to work even harder.

A PAINTING IN EACH POEM — WANG WEI

Wang Wei (AD 701–761) was a man of many talents and was known for his poetry, painting, music and calligraphy. He was one of the representative figures of bucolic poetry during the High Tang period. Like Tao Yuanming before him, he employed simple and plain language to express deep meanings. His poetry is lyrical and vivid, like a painting. The Song Dynasty poet, Su Shi, admired his poetry, remarking that "there is a painting in each poem". Wang Wei's poems cover a wide range of subject matters, but he is best known for his bucolic and landscape poems that constitute the bulk of his poetic oeuvre.

Selected Poems of Wang Wei

Mountain Lodge in Autumn Twilight
In the empty mountain after a fresh rain,
The air feels more like autumn at dusk.
Bright moon through pines shine,
Clear spring over stones flow.
Bamboo rustles as girls return from washing,
Lotus stirs as a fishing boat glides.
The fragrance of spring is fading,
Yet, friend, you can linger here still.

The poem depicts an autumn evening and the joys of the rural life and landscape. Packed with clear and sharp images, the poem is like a piece of landscape.

Thinking of My Brothers in Shandong at the Double Ninth Festival

A lonely roamer in a strange place,
At each festival more homesick I feel.
Now my brothers must be high in a mountain,
Sighing over me though dogwood branches fair.

This is a poem on homesickness. The line — "At each festival more homesick I feel" — clearly evokes the feeling of a traveller far from home, and it has thus become a popular saying.

Yearning

Red love peas in the southern lands,
Grow in sprigs when spring comes.
Please pick more, I ask,
They're the best keepsake for love and longing.

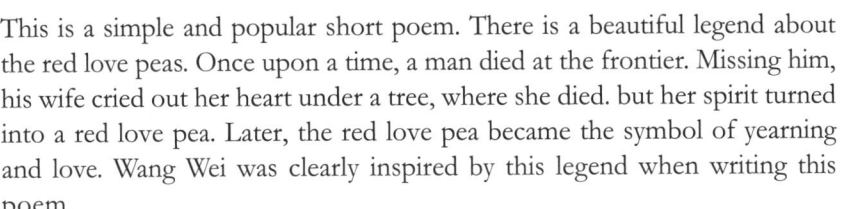

This is a simple and popular short poem. There is a beautiful legend about the red love peas. Once upon a time, a man died at the frontier. Missing him, his wife cried out her heart under a tree, where she died. but her spirit turned into a red love pea. Later, the red love pea became the symbol of yearning and love. Wang Wei was clearly inspired by this legend when writing this poem.

HIGH TANG FRONTIER POETRY

Frontier poetry describes the natural scenery of the border areas and reflects the thoughts and feelings of the soldiers. The Tang Dynasty saw many years of war against the Huns, and many patriotic poets went to the frontline and composed frontier poetry. Though sentimental sometimes, these poems as a whole are bold, unconstrained and optimistic. The best known frontier poets of the Tang Dynasty include Gao Shi, Cen Can, Wang Changling and Wang Han.

Gao Shi (AD 704–765) and Cen Can (AD 715–770)

Gao Shi and Cen Can were good friends with similar backgrounds. Both born into poor families, Gao had fought personally in the front and accumulated much military experience, while Cen Can had also been to the northwestern frontiers twice. With their long observation of and close contact with the border areas and military life, they composed many excellent frontier poems. Their names are often mentioned together in the studies of Chinese literature.

A Farewell to Dongda (I), by Gao Shi (excerpt)

The white sun setting behind the endless yellow clouds,
The north wind blows the wild geese flying in snow flurries.
Do not fear that you will find no friends on the road ahead,
Your name is known through all the land.

Though solemn, the poem is moving and heroic in tone.

A Song of White Snow for Field-Clerk Wu Returning to the Capital, Cen Can (excerpt)

The north wind sweeps the land and breaks the grasses,
August now, but a snow is falling across the Tartar sky.
Like a blast of spring wind in the night,
Thousands of pear trees come into full bloom suddenly.

The poem portrays two friends parting in the snowy frontiers. The natural scenes delineated match perfectly the sentiments expressed.

Wang Changling (AD 698–757)

Wang Changling is hailed as a grand master of seven-character quatrains. Using fresh and spontaneous language to express profound, graceful and veiled sentiments, most of his poems deal with frontier fortresses, life on horseback and complaints from the border.

Leaving the Fortress on a Mission

The moon of the Qin Dynasty and the pass of the Han period,
And the troops have not yet returned from a long march.
But as long as the Winged General defends the Dragon City,
Not a single Tartar horseman will cross the Yin Mountains!

The poem voices the brave sentiments of the border troops. The Winged General Li Guang of the Han Dynasty is invoked to show the poet's concern over the situation at the frontier.

Wang Han (years of birth and death unknown)

Wang Han left only a few poems, but he won lasting fame with the poem, 'A Song of Liangzhou'.

A Song of Liangzhou

Goblets of luminous jade brimming with sweet wine,
We want to have a swig when urgent tunes of lutes rise.
Please don't laugh when we fall drunk on the battleground,
How many soldiers have returned alive since olden times?

Here, the poem portrays a group of soldiers leaving on a mission, the last line evoking their bleak uncertainty whether they would be able to return.

THE DEITY OF POETRY — LI BAI

Li Bai (AD 701–762)

Li Bai, alias Taibai, was the foremost poet of the High Tang period. He wrote more than a thousand poems in his life and has been acclaimed as the Deity of Poetry. Gallant in nature, Li Bai loved drinking, swordplay and travel. The vicissitudes of his life provided rich inspiration for his poetry. His poems are bold and unfettered in character and filled with passion. He epitomises the spirit of the High Tang period.

Selected Poems by Li Bai

Reflections on a Quiet Night
Before my bed the moonlight shines,
Like hoarfrost on the ground.
Raising my head, I look at the bright moon;
Hanging my head, I think of home.

The poem describes homesickness in a moonlit night. It is easy, clear and beautiful. Many Chinese children know this verse by heart.

Farewell to Secretary Li Yun At Xie Tiao Pavilion in Xuanzhou (excerpt)
Try to stop the water with a sword, yet it still flows,
Attempt to dispel sorrow with wine, yet it grows.
If I cannot fulfill my ambitions in this world,
Why not untie my hair and depart in a skiff tomorrow?

In this poem, the poet expresses his disillusionment with his failure in a career as an official and his indignation because he could find no way to serve the country. At the same time, he expressed his determination to leave and lead a wandering life. Bold and unconstrained in tone, Li Bai's voice comes through clearly in his poetry.

Bring in the Wine (excerpt)

Don't you see the Yellow River pouring out of the sky,
and rumbling towards the ocean never to return?
Don't you see a man grieving before a bright mirror in the hall over his locks
That has turned from black in the morning to snow-white in the evening?
You should have a good time when you are blessed with some success,
And not raise your gold goblets empty to the moon.
My talent was given by heaven, and will surely be put to use,
A thousand gold coins, spent now, will come back in the end.

Here the poet expresses his pent-up resentment about his unfulfilled ambitions. Yet he did not give up hope and instead remained confident.

Farewell to a Friend

Green ridges stand outside the north wall,
and a gleaming river girdles the eastern city.
Here we bid adieu to each other,
You'll start a long journey as lonely duckweed.
A traveller wanders like a floating cloud,
And the sunset lingers like a friend long lost.
Waving to each other, we start to leave,
The horses neigh sadly and reluctantly.

Li Bai cherished friendship dearly. He wrote many moving poems on friendship, filled with profound and sincere emotions, as in this poem of farewell to a friend.

A Story of Li Bai

Li Bai did not like to study as a child. One day, when he was playing truant, he met an old woman grinding an iron pestle on his way home.

Grandma, what are you doing that for?

I want to grind the pestle into an embroidery needle.

The pestle is so thick. When will you be able to grind it into a needle?

As long as I persist, I will make it sooner or later.

Inspired by the old woman's words, Li Bai realized that he should persevere in his studies and not give up halfway. From then on, he worked hard at his studies.

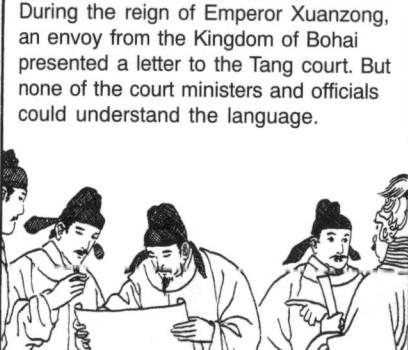

During the reign of Emperor Xuanzong, an envoy from the Kingdom of Bohai presented a letter to the Tang court. But none of the court ministers and officials could understand the language.

Your Majesty, it is said that Li Bai knows this language.

Send for him quickly!

Your Majesty, the letter demands that we should cede territories to them, or they will attack us. Allow me to write a reply. I will use the carrot and the stick to induce the Kingdom of Bohai to submit to our empire.

Men, prepare the four treasures of the study for dear scholar Li so that he can write a reply.

When I took the Highest Imperial Civil Service Examination, I failed because of the tricks played by the Chief Examiner Yang Guozhong and Eunuch Gao Lishi.

Why not take this chance to make fun of them?

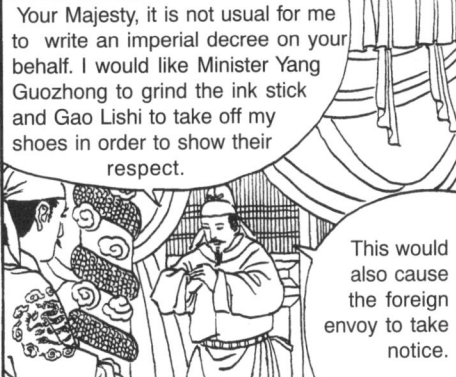

Your Majesty, it is not usual for me to write an imperial decree on your behalf. I would like Minister Yang Guozhong to grind the ink stick and Gao Lishi to take off my shoes in order to show their respect.

This would also cause the foreign envoy to take notice.

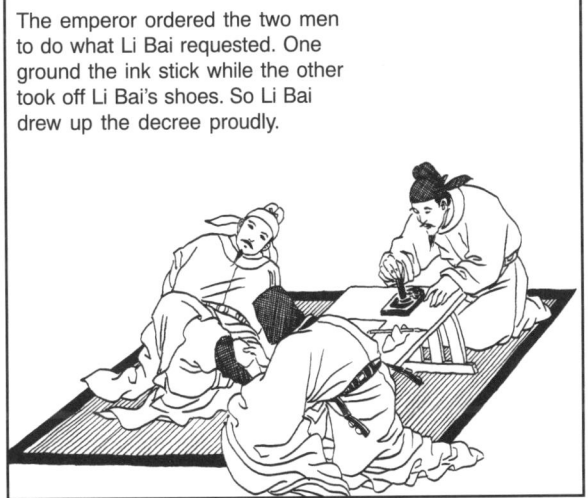

The emperor ordered the two men to do what Li Bai requested. One ground the ink stick while the other took off Li Bai's shoes. So Li Bai drew up the decree proudly.

Impressed, the envoy returned to report to the King of Bohai, and thereafter, the kingdom came under Tang rule.

THE SAGE OF POETRY — DU FU

Du Fu (AD 712–770)

Du Fu's fame matches Li Bai's, and he is known as the Sage of Poetry. Born into a family of poets, he started to compose poems when he was seven years old. A prolific poet, Du Fu has more than 1,400 poems to his name. His years of wandering gave him insight into the sufferings of the common people. Deep concern for his country and people runs through his poetry which reflect the conditions of his time and are often termed 'historical poems'. His sunset years were passed in poverty, and he died of illness in a boat on the Xiang River at the age of 59.

Famous lines by Du Fu

Spring View

The state has fallen apart, yet the mountains and rivers still remain,
It is spring now in the city, and weeds and trees are growing wild.
Lamenting the troubled times, I am in tears even before flowers,
Hating to part, I am startled even by the chittering birds.
The beacon-fires have been burning for three months in a row,
And a letter from home is worth thousands of gold coins.
Stroked constantly, my grey hair has become so thin,
Hardly can it hold even a small object like a hairpin.

Here in this poem we are presented with a bleak scene — a country ravaged and families torn apart by war. Through this, the poet expressed his love for his country and longing for home.

Inside the vermilion gates wine and meat spoil,
Along the road outside lie the bones of men frozen to death.

Seeing the rich squander their wealth on wine and pleasure while the poor had to suffer from coldness and hunger, Du Fu indignantly wrote these enduring lines. The couplet delivers a strong complaint on behalf of the poor and exploited people.

Officers in Shihao Village

Du Fu's most famous poems are those dealing with the Rebellion of An Lushan and Shi Siming (AD 755–763) which brought enormous suffering to the common folk. His representative works in this area include the three poems on officers (set respectively in Xin'an, Tonguan and Shihao) and three parting poems (on newlyweds, the aged and the homeless). Here is the story told in 'Officers in Shihao Village'.

One day Du Fu lodged at a villager's home in Shihao Village.

At midnight, officers came to press-gang able-bodied men.

The grandfather hurriedly climbed over the wall and hid himself.

My three sons have all been drafted. Two of them have died on the battlefield. Now only my daughter-in-law, my grandchild and I are left. If you insist, please allow me, an old woman, to go and cook for you.

Somebody is better than nobody. Come with us!

Sob... sob...

The Rebellion of An Lushan and Shi Siming

During the mid-Tang period, Governor An Lushan of Pinglu and his adjunct Shi Siming launched a rebellion and advanced with hundreds of thousands of troops to attack Luoyang and Chang'an, two administrative centers of the Tang government. This was the Rebellion of An Lushan and Shi Siming. They were both Tartar generals serving the Tang government. Through Lady Yang, Emperor Xuanzong's beloved concubine, An Lushan gained the emperor's favor. Granted supreme power, he committed all kinds of outrages in the areas under his jurisdiction.

A Story of Du Fu

Du Fu offended some high-ranking officials with his critical poems on behalf of the people. He was thus banished by the emperor to the countryside.

He came to the bank of Huanhua Brook and settled down in a thatched cottage. Sitting by a stump, he was so hungry and tired that he fell asleep unawares.

Mr Du Fu, you have written so many poems to speak for us poor people.

We are also concerned about you!

Thank you all.

The common folk came and brought him some food.

So, Du Fu settled down there, growing melons and gathering wild garlic with the people.

In his free time, he continued to study and write poems. Later, the cottage that he lived in became known as Du Fu Cottage.

MID-TANG POETS

Ten Talents of Dali

During the Dali period under Emperor Daizong, there was a group of prominent poets such as Liu Changqing, Gu Kuang and Wei Yingwu, who were known as the "Ten Talents of Dali". However, their works were largely unremarkable.

Meng Jiao (AD 751–814)

One of the highly acclaimed poets of the mid-Tang period, Meng Jiao is the author of 'A Traveller's Song', an ode to loving mothers that has been widely read for over one thousand years. The poem tells of a mother sewing clothes for her son, who is planning a long journey, thus showing the great and profound love of a mother.

A Traveller's Song

Threads in the hands of a loving mother,
Clothes for her son planning a long journey.
Carefully and thoroughly she sews and mends,
Fearing that he may be long away.
Who said the heart of a blade of grass
Can repay the light of the spring sun?

Liu Yuxi (AD 772–842)

Due to setbacks in his political career, Liu Yuxi was banished to minor posts in Langzhou and other places. In 'Black-Dress Lane', he explored the vicissitudes of history using swallows as a metaphor.

Black-Dress Lane

By the Bridge of Vermilion Fowls weeds and flowers run wild,
at the end of Black-Dress Lane the evening sun shines obliquely.
In times past, swallows visited noble houses like Wang's and Xie's,
yet now they make their nests on the roofs of ordinary people.

Liu Zongyuan (AD 773–819)

Liu Zongyuan is both a great prose writer and a noted poet. He is good at writing travel accounts and landscape poems.

Snow-Covered River

Amidst a thousand mountains not a single bird is seen,
and along ten thousand paths no footprint discovered;
On a lone boat, wearing a bamboo cloak, an old man
Is fishing alone in the cold snow-covered river.

Li He (AD 790–816)

Li He was an ill-starred child prodigy. Although he established his nationwide reputation with 'Ode to the Prefect of Yanmen' at the age of 18, he had never taken any official post in his lifetime. He lived only 26 years, and told his mother on his deathbed that the Jade Emperor, who, having just built a palace, invited him to go there and write essays.

Li He's Bag of Poems

Li He used to roam about riding on the back of a donkey. He always took a bag with him. Whenever he thought of any good poetic lines, he would write them down on a sheet of paper and then put it in the bag. Back at home, he would stay up a whole night sorting out the lines. Seeing this, his mother felt rather worried, "Son, you are working out your heart over your poems! When will you have a rest?"

Jia Dao (AD 779–843)

Jia Dao's most popular poem is 'A Failed Visit to a Recluse'. Written in a spontaneous style, the poem vividly sketches the poet's disappointment at his failure to meet the recluse.

A Failed Visit to a Recluse

To my question the child beneath the pines replied:
My teacher has gone to collect medicinal herbs.
I'm sure he's in the mountain,
Yet the clouds are so thick, I cannot tell exactly where.

A Story of "Push" and "Knock"

Birds nestling in trees by the pond, / a monk pushing a door under the moon. 'Push' doesn't seem right, how about 'knock'?

Jia Dao

Push... knock... push... knock...

Han Yu, then a high-ranking official in the capital, happened to be passing by with his retinue.

Hey, why are you blocking the way?

Oh! Sorry, I was thinking about the words of a poem. I didn't mean to hit you.

Jia Dao told Han Yu what he had been mulling over.

I feel that 'knock' is more appropriate.

In the moonlight, with birds sleeping in the trees by the pond, it is quiet all around. 'Knock' would produce a sound and thus give the effect of "sound in silence".

Besides, this happens in the still of night. The door should be closed. You can't 'push' it open. So, it is better to 'knock'.

Sir, what a cogent explanation you have offered!

From then on, Jia Dao and Han Yu became close friends in poetry and prose. The phrase "push and knock" also became a common term for weighing every word.

65

BAI JUYI — "THIS SORROW GOES ON AND ON FOREVER"

Bai Juyi (AD 772–846)

Bai Juyi is the greatest poet of the mid-Tang period. He is the most prolific poet of the Tang Dynasty and over three thousand of his poems survive. A realist poet, Bai Juyi felt that poetry should reflect reality, as well as express and guide popular sentiment. He initiated the Movement of New Ballad-Songs of Yuefu (Bureau of Music) with the aim to learn from folksongs modes of expression and the principle of emphasizing the reality. His most famous poetic works are two long narrative poems — 'Song of Unending Sorrow' and 'Song of the *Pipa*'.

Selected Poems by Bai Juyi

Grasses

Grasses spreading over the plain,
Flourish and wither each year.
Burnt but not destroyed by prairie fires,
They sprout again when spring winds blow.

Bai Juyi's unusual talent was already evident from childhood. He wrote the above poem when he was only 16. Once he went to visit a poet named Gu Kuang with a volume of his poems, telling Gu that he was going to the capital city to attend the Imperial Civil Service Examination and wanted the poet's opinion. Gu Kuang said at the time, "Your name is Bai Juyi? Juyi, Juyi, well, it won't be easy to establish yourself in Chang'an ,where even rice is expensive." Then, he opened Bai Juyi's book of poems and came across 'Grasses'. Amazed, Gu Kuang immediately corrected himself, declaring, "It won't be that difficult for you, considering your talent!"

Song of Unending Sorrow

'Song of Undending Sorrow' is a moving narrative poem about the love between Emperor Xuanzong and his beloved concubine, Lady Yang.

The poem relates how Lady Yang outshone all the court ladies. "When she glanced back with a smile, a hundred spells were cast, And all powdered and painted faces of the Six Palaces faded into nothing."

The emperor was so infatuated with her that though "There were other ladies in his court, three thousand of rare beauty, But his favors to three thousand were concentrated in one body."

However, such happy times did not last long. A rebellion broke out and the emperor fled the court with his harem.

Many generals and soldiers blamed the rebellion on Lady Yang and demanded that she be executed. The emperor had no way but to order her to commit suicide.

When the rebellion was put down, the emperor returned to the imperial court and missed Lady Yang terribly.

A Taoist monk offered to go and look for her. He came to an enchanted mountain in the sea.

Among the many beautiful immortals in the mountain, he saw one who looked very much like Lady Yang, by the name of "Yang Taizhen". She asked him to bring her gifts to the emperor.

Please tell His Majesty not to forget what we said to each other secretly in the night, in the Palace of Eternal Life on the seventh day of the Seventh-month: "We wish to fly in heaven like two birds wing to wing and to grow together on the earth like two intertwined branches."

Heaven and earth endure, but both will come to an end someday. In contrast, the sorrow of the emperor and Lady Yang at their parting will go on forever.

LATE TANG POETS — LI AND DU JUNIOR

Historically, the late Tang period spans about seven to eight decades, from the reign of Emperor Wenzong through the fall of the dynasty. The once-flourishing Tang Dynasty entered a state of decline, and the grandeur and optimism of the High Tang period gave way to laments about the times and the world. Among the poets of this era, the most oustanding are Li Shangyin and Du Mu. Their status in the Late Tang period are comparable to that of Li Bai and Du Fu during the High Tang period, hence they are termed Li and Du Junior.

Li Shangyin (AD 813–858)

In the early part of his writing career Li Shangyin was concerned about political affairs and wrote a number of poems on social reality. Later, setbacks in his official career caused a turn: he started to lament his personal unpleasant experiences in his poems in a downcast and pathetic tone. Written in elegant language and filled with deep and sincere feelings, his love poems are the most famous and also the most popular in his poetic oeuvre. "Sunset is beautiful beyond words, / yet dusk is coming nigh" is a household couplet from one of his poems.

Untitled

To meet is hard, and to part even harder,
East wind fading and flowers withered.
A spring silkworm spins threads till death,
A candle dries its tears only when burned out.
Morning mirror reveals my fair hair sadly changed,
Reading at night you can feel the chill moonlight.
It isn't a long way to Penglai fairyland from here,
Would the blue bird could be our faithful courier.

This is a touching poem on a couple of lovers parting from each other. "A spring silkworm spins threads till death, /A candle dries its tears only when burned out" express their unwavering commitment to love.

Du Mu (AD 803–852)

A man born of a good family, Du Mu maintained a lifelong concern about socio-political affairs. Based often on his reflections on historical events and his close examination of social reality, his poetic works reveal his anxiety over the future of the empire, his troubled feelings about the declining society and his sorrow over his powerlessness to reverse the situation.

Passing Huaqing Palace

Looking from Chang'an, the plants there look like brocades,
At the peak thousands of gates, one by one, open.
A horse galloping in red dust and the concubine smiling,
Nobody knows that the carrier of lychees is coming.

Here the poet satirizes the ruler's extravagant and dissipated life in a veiled but pungent style.

CLASSICAL PROSE MOVEMENT

Beside poetry, Tang Dynasty also witnessed the flourishing of many other literary styles. In the realm of prose, the Classical Prose Movement headed by Han Yu emphasised the unity of composition and morality and wanted a return to Confucian ethics and the tradition of Pre-Qin prose, while at the same time denouncing the aesthetic parallel prose established since the Six Dynasties. Han Yu, Liu Zongyuan and six Song Dynasty prose writers (Ouyang Xiu, Zeng Gong, Wang Anshi, Su Shi, Su Xun and Su Zhe)were later known collectively as the "Eight Prose Masters of the Tang and Song Dynasties."

Han Yu (AD 768–824)

Han Yu wrote many prose classics, such as *Postscript to the Biography of Zhang Xun*, *In Memory of My Nephew*, *An Inquiry into the Way* and *Of Teachers*. Su Shi, a great man of letters in the Song Dynasty, praised Han Yu's compositions as "rising from the declining eight dynasties."

An Adapted Essay by Han Yu

Random Words

Bo Le, the horse expert, comes before any excellent steed in the world. Excellent steeds are numerous, whereas an expert like Bo Le is hard to find.

Though there are good horses indeed, most of them are subject to the insults of slaves and die with their value unrecognised.

A short-sighted stableman points his whip at an excellent steed, declaring, "There are no good horses in the world!"
Is it true that no good horses exist? Or is it because he cannot recognize them?

The Story of Han Yu

Han Yu came to Chang'an to take the Imperial Civil Service Examination at 23. Pleased with his essay, he believed he would certainly pass, but was given a failing grade.

It turned out that most scholars of that time favoured parallel prose, focusing on rhymes, rhythms, couplets and literary allusions, while neglecting content. Disdaining parallel prose, Han Yu had written in a natural, expressive style. The chief examiner, Lu Zhi took a look at his essay and brushed it aside.

The exam question is the same as last year. I might as well simply copy what I wrote last time and hand it in.

Han Yu came for the exam again the following year.

This candidate failed last time. How dare he hand in the same essay?

I didn't read it carefully last time. I'll take it seriously this time.

After reading Han Yu's essay closely, the examiner was impressed. Han Yu was thus granted the title of *Jinshi* (a successful candidate in the highest imperial examination).

Soon after his official career started, Han Yu launched a prose reform movement, or rather, the Classical Prose Movement.

Liu Zongyuan (AD 773–819)

Besides his accomplishments as a poet Liu Zongyan was also an active supporter of the Classical Prose Movement. He wrote excellent prose accounts of his excursions into nature, among which the best-known is *Eight Landscape Essays Written in Yongzhou.* He is also an accomplished writer of allegorical essays

A Donkey in Guizhou

TALES OF THE TANG DYNASTY

Most tales of the Tang Dynasty were fantastic stories and anecdotes. With gripping and complicated plots, vivid characters and lively narration, they represent the coming of age for Chinese fiction. In terms of subject matter, some are romances dealing with talents and beauties, like "The Tale of Hua Xiaoyu" and "Miss Li Wa", while others featured heroes weeding out the wicked, such as "The Curly-Bearded Stranger" and "Miss Hongxian".

Adapted Tales of the Tang Dynasty:

The Prefect of Nanke

A man named Chun-yu Fen was drunk and passed out beneath a tree. He dreamt of two men in purple.

We are messengers from the State of Huai'an. Our king has sent us here to welcome you.

Chun-yu Fen climbed onto their chariot. Amazingly, the vehicle rushed towards a big locust tree and entered a hole in it.

After an audience with the King, Chun-yu Fen was married to the princess and granted the title of Prefect of Nanke County.

After twenty years in office, he was banished by the king when he lost a battle with a neighbouring state.

On waking, he found himself lying beside an anthill under a locust tree. The anthill must have been the State of Huai'an in his dream.

Tales of the Tang Dynasty:

The Story of Liu Yi

I am Dragon Girl of Dongting Lake. After I married Little Dragon of Jing River, he and his mother treated me very cruelly. Please carry a message to my father.

Liu Yi had failed in the Imperial Service Examination. He met a shepherdess on his way home.

Hearing this, Liu felt very indignant and promised to help her out.

When the Dragon King heard of this, he sent Lord Qiantang to rescue Dragon Girl.

Lord Qiantang wanted to marry Dragon Girl to Liu Yi, but Liu rejected the proposal sternly because of his arrogant tone.

Liu Yi went home and married a Miss Lu from Fanyang. It turned out in the end that his wife was actually Dragon Girl incarnate.

A *Ci* Poet Among the Flowers — Wen Tingyun

Wen Tingyun (ca. AD 812–866)

A scholar living in the late Tang period, Wen Tingyun is the first established *Ci* writer. Most of his *Ci* poems relate love affairs, and describe women's garments and postures in an ornate and flowery style. That is why he is titled a *Ci* writer "among the flowers."

Wen Tingyun is also known as a fast *Ci* writer. It was said that he never wrote drafts. He simply sat at a desk with each hand tucked into the opposite sleeve, thinking for a short while and crossing his hands eight times before writing a *Ci* in a flash.

Among the Flowers

Zhao Chongzuo of the Late Shu Dynasty during the Five Dynasties and Ten Kingdoms period collected five hundred *Ci* poems by eighteen literati of the time, compiling them into an anthology called *Among the Flowers*. Most of the pieces are devoted to romantic entanglements and the lives of the upper-class in an ornate style. That is also why these poets were labelled "poets among the flowers." Wen Tingyun was the founder of this particular poetic style. The anthology is the earliest and largest collection of *Ci* poems.

> **Tune: Dreaming of the South Side of the River**
> *Having dressed up,*
> *In a riverside tower I stand alone against the railing.*
> *A thousand sails go by but none is the one I wait for.*
> *The evening sun is affectionate and the river gentle,*
> *Gazing at the white-duckweed islet I am heart-broken.*
>
> This *Ci* describes a girl missing her lover and awaiting his return. The line, "A thousand sails go by but none is the one I wait for" demonstrates her devotion to her love.

THE POET EMPEROR — LI YU

Li Yu (AD 937–978)
Following the end of the Tang Dynasty was the period in
China known as the Five Dynasties and Ten Kingdoms (AD
907–979). The last emperor of the Southern Tang Dynasty
was the great poet, Li Yu. When the regime was defeated
by the Song army, Li Yu was taken prisoner and eventually
poisoned by Emperor Taizong of the Song Dynasty.

Though a poor ruler, Li Yu was a first-rate poet. His best works were written
following the collapse of his dynasty. Written in a simple, elegant and moving
style, these *Ci* poems voice his sentimental attachment to and his deep sorrow
over his lost country. Many famous lines are drawn from his poems, such as
"Our lives are an endless sorrow like rivers running always to the east" and
"Tell me — how much is your sorrow? / Like a spring river flowing eastwards
endlessly."

> **Tune: The Beauty of Yu**
> *Spring flowers and harvest moon, when will they fade?*
> *How much of past events do I still remember?*
> *To my chamber last night came again the east wind,*
> *I cannot bear to look back on my lost country under the bright moon.*
>
> *The carved balustrades and jade-inlaid steps should still be there,*
> *Only faces are changed.*
> *Tell me—how much is your sorrow?*
> *Like a spring river flowing eastwards endlessly.*
>
> This is Li Yu's masterpiece, an outpouring of his true feelings as a prisoner
> of the Song Dynasty.

Born by Mistake into an Imperial Family —
The Story of Li Yu

The Song army conquered Southern Tang and Li Yu was taken prisoner. Emperor Taizu of the Song Dynasty held a banquet for his ministers and generals. He invited Li Yu as well.

I hear you're a talented poet. Please recite some poems to liven up the banquet!

Ok, I'll recite one...

Very good indeed!

If you had ruled as well as you had worked on your werse, you wouldn't have ended up like this today.

During his imprisonment Li Yu felt extremely sad whenever he thought of his lost country. He wrote many nostalgic *Ci* poems on the topic.

This came to the ears of Emperor Taizong of the Song Dynasty, the successor to Emperor Taizu.

Li Yu still thinks of his country. We must not keep him around.

So, the emperor sent a bottle of poisoned wine to Li Yu and killed him.

Some Basic Poetry Terms

Terms used to describe poetic forms include tetrasyllabic lines, pentasyllabic lines and heptasyllabic lines, quatrains and octaves.

Poems of tetrasyllabic lines have four Chinese characters to each line, for example: "I wonder while drinking, /How long we live?"

Pentasyllabic-line poems refer to poems which have lines consisting of five Chinese characters, for example: "Springtime sleeper knows no dawn,/ Birds heard chittering all around."

Poems in heptasyllabic lines are poems with seven Chinese characters in each line, for example: "A lonely stranger in a strange place, / All the more homesick whenever festivals fall."

Mixed poems refer to poems made up of lines of different lengths, for example: "Goose, goose, goose, / Bending your neck skywards you sing."

An octave refers to a poem comprising eight lines.

A quatrain refers to a four-line poem.

Octaves and quatrains also have strict rules on the number of characters per line or lines per poem, and rhymes and rhythms.

Classsical-style poetry is freer and more flexible as it does not specify the number of characters, lines and metrical patterns.

What is *Ci*?

Also known as tunes, lyrics or poems of long and short lines, *Ci* refers originally to lyrics to be sung at banquets.

The varied tunes determine the irregular lines of lyrics.

Ci can be sung to different tunes. Each tune has a unique name, such as 'Beautiful Barbarians' and 'Mulberry Picking'.

Each tune is subject to fixed rules regarding rhythms, rhymes and the number of lines and characters per line.

Poets write lyrics in strict accordance with tunes and beats.

LITERATURE OF THE SONG DYNASTY

As in the Tang Dynasty, Chinese literature flourished during the Song Dynasty. Song literature has its own distinct character. If Tang literature is vibrant, with a youthful spirit like the bright springtime, then Song literature seems more mature, like a bumper harvest in the autumn. During the Southern Song Dynasty, the northern part of China fell into the hands of the ethnic Jin (Jin Dynasty). It was a dream of Song scholar-officials for several centuries to recover the lost territory. As a result, a solemn and stirring patriotism pervades the literature of this period.

LEADING LIGHT OF EARLY SONG LITERATURE — OUYANG XIU

Ouyang Xiu (1007–1072)

A foremost literary figure of the early Song period, Ouyang Xiu was an advocate of the Classical Prose Movement. During the reign of Emperor Renzong, Ouyang Xiu presided over the highest imperial examination as a grand *Hanlin* Academy scholar and stipulated that all test takers should write in plain language. The unknown talents he found and nurtured in this way include Su Shi, Su Zhe, Su Xun and Wang Anshi, who would later become influential literati.

Selected *Ci* by Ouyang Xiu

> **Tune: The Butterfly woos the Blossoms**
> *Deep and deep is the courtyard confined,*
> *Willows are dense as smoke,*
> *Screens and curtains are drawn everywhere.*
> *Jade gag-bit and carved saddle seen outside the brothel,*
> *High walls block the sight of the merry-making street.*
> *Wind is rough and rain heavy in late March,*
> *Dusk is shut out by the door,*
> *Yet no way for me to delay the spring.*
> *Inquire the flowers with teary eyes but get no answer,*
> *Withered blossoms are wafted over the swing.*
>
> This *Ci* depicts a lonely woman whose philandering husband spends most of his time everyday in brothels. So, the teary woman can only confide her troubles to the blossoms, which of course cannot understand.

The tippler's heart is not in the cup but in the landscape

Ouyang Xiu styled himself as "the old tippler". In his masterpiece, 'Record of the Old Tippler's Pavilion', he described the beautiful scenery around the district of Chu and his personal delight in the landscape. The line, "The tippler's heart is not in the cup but in the landscape" later developed into an idiom to refer to a man with ulterior motives.

The Story of Ouyang Xiu

Ouyang Xiu was born into a poor family. His father died when he was four, so his mother took the children to their uncle, then working as an official in Suizhou.

His mother often told them stories about how their father had been an upright and honest man, thus teaching them morals.

They could not afford paper, so the mother wrote on the ground with sticks in order to teach her child.

Whenever he came across any good poems, he would learn them by heart, either through copying or through reciting.

When Ouyang Xiu grew older, his mother started to teach him how to read poetry. As they did not have money for books, Ouyang Xiu would borrow books from the large private collection of a family named Li in the southern part of the town.

Thanks to the careful teaching of his mother and his personal efforts, Ouyang Xiu eventually became a leader of the literary community in the early Song Dynasty.

Ci Writers in the Early Song Period

Fan Zhongyan (989–1052)

Fan Zhongyan was both a leader of political reforms and an outstanding writer in the early Northern Song period. He left behind only a few *Ci* poems, most of them dealing with social reality.

Be worried before anyone else and enjoy life only after everyone else finds enjoyment

This famous sentence comes from his classic essay, 'Account of Yueyang Pavilion'. The essay reveals his lofty ideals and noble feelings that the whole nation is his personal responsibility, as well as his concern for the country and the people.

Yan Shu (991–1055)

A child prodigy, Yan Shu started to write poems at seven and attended the Imperial Examination at 13. Highly regarded by Emperor Zhenzong, he held high-ranking official posts both in the capital and in the provinces. Most of his *Ci* poems deal with the leisurely life of the noble class, in particular romances.

Tune: Washing Gauge by the River
A new lyric composed and a goblet of wine downed,
The weather's same as last year and so is the pavilion.
The sun is setting and when will you return?
Nothing I can do but sigh over the fallen blossoms.
The swallows, like acquiantances, returning,
I linger alone on a fragrant garden path.

Fan Zhongyan Forces Himself
to Eat Pickles and Porridge

Fan Zhongyan was very poor. He would cook a pot of porridge and divide it into four portions, which he ate with pickles to fill his stomach from day to night.

Brother Fan, my father saw how you were living. He asked me to bring you some wine and dishes.

Thank you very much.

Why did he put them aside?

Why don't you eat? Is the food not good enough for you?

No, not at all!

What worries me is that if I enjoy these delicacies now, I won't be able to stand eating porridge again.

Liu Yong (ca. 987–1053)

Before Liu Yong, most *Ci* poems were short. He composed many long ones to slow-paced tunes. His works were very popular, and could be heard as far as Xi Xia. He spent most of his time in wine shops and teahouses, composing *Ci* for songstresses, who held him in high esteem. When he died in poverty, they raised funds for his burial. Each year, during the (Clear and Bright) Qing Ming Festival, these songstresses would gather at his tomb for a memorial ceremony.

Tune: Rain-soaked Bell (excerpt)

Lovers from of old have grieved over parting,
More so in this cold autumn season!
Where shall I be when I wake from my drink this evening?
Willow banks, the morning breeze, a waning moon.
I'll be away for years,
Fine moments and enchanting scenes will mean nothing.
Even if I possess a thousand romantic sentiments,
To whom can I impart them now?

The poem presents a scene of lovers parting. Infused with a sense of deep sorrow and reminiscence, the wistful imagery of willows, the morning breeze and waning moon add to the lonely and sad atmosphere.

Wang Anshi (1021–1086)

Also a noted statesman, Wang Anshi married his political ideals to his literary works. Wang's best-known *Ci* is 'Fragrant Laurel Branch' or 'Meditating on the Past at Jinling (present-day Nanjing)'

Tune: Fragrant Laurel Branch (excerpt)

Thinking of the years spent pursuing luxuries
Outside the gate and in those pavilions, sorrow and hatred together unending.
Since ancient times, thinking back on this lofty place,
Scholars have lamented the past honour and disgrace.
Events of the Six Dynasties have gone with the river,
Only chill smoke and withered grasses remain.
Even now, the songstresses still sing
The old tune, 'Blossoms in the Backyard'.

Here, the poet meditated on the past and condemned those rulers who indulged in merrymaking while neglecting administrative matters.

The Greatest Writer of the Song Dynasty — Su Shi

Su Shi (1037–1101)

The greatest writer of the Song Dynasty, Su Shi is also known as Su Dongpo. Su Shi, his father Su Xun and his brother Su Zhe are known as the Three Sus.

Due to differences in opinion on government with Wang Anshi, who was then in charge of government affairs, Su Shi was banished many times. These political setbacks enabled him to travel widely and visit famous scenic locations such as reputed mountains and major rivers. At the same time, he also had the opportunity to come into contact with the lower social strata and understand the sufferings of ordinary people. The ups and downs of life had not defeated this bold and free-spirited poet. Rather, they widened his vision and enriched his experiences for his later literary achievements.

Su Shi achieved success in many literary fields. Numbered among the Eight Prose Masters of the Tang and Song Dynasties, his prose writings are vigorous, unrestrained and spontaneous. His masterpiece, "Red Cliff", is widely recognised as an immortal work in ancient Chinese literature. His bold and open *Ci* poems liberated the poetic form from the narrow subjects of love, separation and nostalgia and propelled it onto a wider plane of nature and society. His *Ci* masterpieces include 'Charming Nian-Nu—Meditating on the Past at Red Cliff' and 'Water Music Prelude'.

How did Su Shi study?

The theme of Su Shi's study habits is, "Read more books, reread them, copy them and think them over." He developed a reading method called "being surrounded on eight sides." This refers to his habit of classifying a book, dividing it into many parts and reading them paragraph by paragraph with different aims.

Famous *Ci* Poems of Su Shi:

Tune: Storm Ceasing

Listen not to the rain pattering on the leaves,
We may as well walk slowly and sing heartily.
Bamboo staff, straw sandals, better than the horseback,
Anything else I fear?
I won't care if I spend my life amidst the misty rain.

Sobered up from delirium by the vernal wind chill,
I feel a bit cold.
The slanting sun is awaiting me at the hilltop.
One more look at the bleak place behind,
I am leaving,
Scarcely disturbed by weather fine or rough.

This Ci poem expresses Su Shi's optimistic and transcendental outlook on setbacks and adverse situations in life.

Tune: Song of River City

For ten years the living and the dead were separated.
To forget I tried,
But never that worked.
Your lonely grave is thousands of miles away,
Nowhere can I tell my sorrow.
Even if we meet now you could never recognize me,
Dust on my face,
Hair like frost.

Last night in a dream I returned home.
By the window,
Were you dressing up.
We gazed at each other speechless,
Tears streaming down our cheeks.
Each year I think of that heart-breaking place:
Moonlit night,
And the ridge of short pines.

This is a moving elegy dedicated to the poet's deceased wife, brimming over with his boundless memory.

The Charms of Nian-Nu — Meditating on the Past at Red Cliff

Eastwards flows this mighty river,
Sweeping away heroes of all ages.
West of the old fortress,
People say,
Is General Zhou's Red Cliff in the Three Kingdoms Period.
Jagged rocks pierce the clouds,
Billows pound the banks,
Throwing up a thousand drifts of snow.
Picturesque is the scene,
And numerous are the heroes.
Recall those years when General Zhou were
Just married to Lady Qiao of noble origin,
What a gallant and ambitious man he was!
With a feather fan and a silk scarf,
He talked and jested,
When the mighty enemy vanished as smoke.
Touring this historical site in my mind,
Funny I may look for my sentimental heart
As my hair has greyed early for my age.
This life is a dream,
Let me offer this goblet of wine to the moon over the river.

Su Shi's Disciples

Su Shi succeeded Ouyang Xiu as the leader of the Song literary scene with his illustrious achievements. Many men of letters were his friends and sought his instructions. Among them Huang Tingjian and Qin Guan were highly favored by Su Shi.

Qin Guan (1049–1100)

Su Shi had a very high opinion of Qin Guan, believing his talent was comparable to that of Qu Yuan and Song Yu. Qin wrote elegant and graceful *Ci* poems.

Tune: Immortal on the Bridge of Magpies

Delicate clouds magically transforming,
Flying stars passing on sorrows,
They cross secretly the long Milky Way.
A meeting amidst golden winds and jade dews,
Is worth many years of conjugal life on earth.
Tender feelings are like water,
The happy date is like a dream,
Reluctantly they look at the bridge of magpies.
With a bond of love that endures,
Need lovers stay close from dawn to dusk?

This poem extols the greatness of pure and sincere love through the mythical love story of the cowherd and the weaving girl who meet each year on the evening of July 7 according to the traditional Chinese calendar.

Su Shi's Younger Sister Tests the Bridegroom

A story written in the Ming Dynasty tells that Su Shi wanted to marry his sister Su Xiaomei to Qin Guan. Being a talented girl, she decided to test the bridegroom on some rhyming couplets on the evening of their marriage.

Su Shi gave Qin Guan some hints, thereby helping him to pass the test. Although this story is not true, it was so popular that many people came to believe that Qin Guan was Su Shi's brother-in-law.

Huang Tingjian (1045–1105)

Huang Tingjian's poetry adheres strictly to formal rules. He was greatly concerned with literary allusions and meter, and founded the Jiangxi School of Poetry.

Tune: Peaceful Joy

Whither has the spring gone?
Bleak all around and no way found.
If you know where spring is,
Call it back to stay with us.
Not a trace is found, heaven knows why.
Go and ask the yellow orioles.
A hundred twitters uttered but none intelligible,
And the wind wafts them over the roses.

This is a poem mourning the end of spring and admonishing people to cherish the prime of their lives rather than let it slip by easily.

Huang Tingjian Pores over Historical Drafts

Huang Tingjian was very serious and meticulous in his work. Once he obtained a volume of the first draft of *A History of the Tang Dynasty*. The draft was dotted with corrections and written in small and blurred characters. Despite this, he pored over the document, copying the corrected parts and comparing them with the original in order to tease out the motives behind the writer's work, learning a great deal in the process.

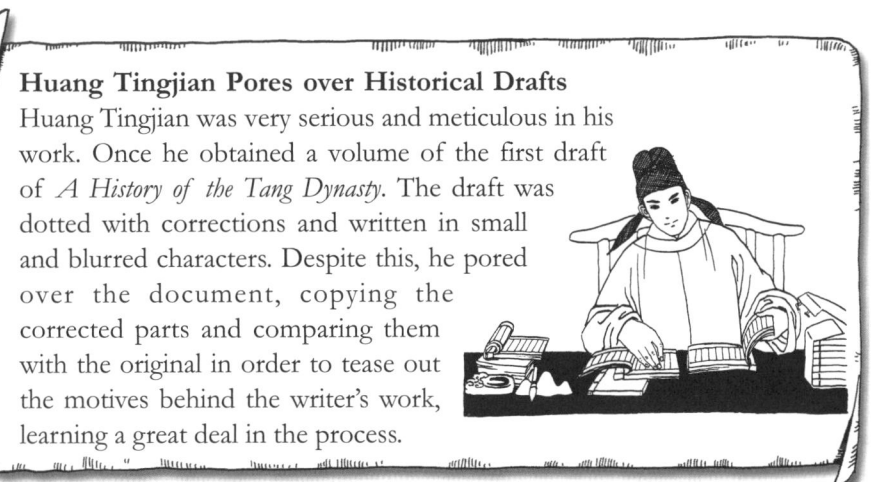

PATRIOTIC POETS

In 1127, the Jin army conquered the Song capital city of Bianjing (present-day Kaifeng in Henan). Emperor Gaozong fled south and established a minor regime in Jiankang (Nanjing). This marked the end of the Northern Song period and the beginning of the Southern Song period. A patriotic tone runs clearly through the literature of this period.

Yue Fei (1103–1142)

The story of the loyal and patriotic General Yue Fei of the Southern Song period is common knowledge. He fought against the invading Jin army for many years, only to be framed and killed by Qin Hui, a treacherous minister. Though not a literatus, Yue Fei was adept with both brush and sword. The few poetic works he left behind are all of high literary value.

Tune: Full River Red

Hair bristling in my helmet, I stand by the railings as the drizzle ends.
I raise my eyes and heave a sigh, emotions seething in my heart.
Fame is but a palmful of dust at the age of 30,
Expeditions of thousands of miles merely a moon in the clouds.
Do not waste your prime; a young man's hair soon turns white, leaving pointless regrets.

The shame hurled on us in the years of Jingkang has yet to be cleansed.
When will our desire for revenge be quenched?
I would drive a chariot to break through Mount Helan.
My lofty ideal is to fill my hunger with Tartar soldiers,
And laugh while tasting the blood of the Huns.
Let's start from scratch, recover the lost territories, and then pay homage to His Majesty.

On a rainy day after routing the Jin army, Yue Fei looked down from a pavilion and composed this heart-stirring classic.

Lu You (1125–1209)

Lu You is one of the best-known patriotic poets in the Southern Song period. Despite repeated setbacks in political career caused by his rivals, Lu You never gave up his patriotic determination to fight the invaders and launch a northern expedition. His poems are filled with a strong longing to serve his nation with his life.

On my grief

Little did I know about the hardship of life in early years,
Looking north to the central plains, I was overwhelmed by mountain-high heroism.
High-decked warships were moored at Guazhou Ferry in night snow,
Armoured steeds galloped out of Dasan Pass against the autumn wind.
My wish to become the Great Wall in the frontier has yet to be fulfilled,
While my hair has already turned grey in the mirror.
What a resounding essay "the Memorial on the Northern Expedition" is!
Nobody is comparable to its writer over the past one thousand years.

Tune: Telling One's True Feelings

That year I travelled thousands of miles for honour,
Defended the border town of Liang-zhou on horseback.
Where did my dream break of passes and rivers?
Dust has darkened my fur coat.

The Tartars are not defeated,
Yet my hair has turned grey,
And tears are shed to no avail.
I have never expected this life:
My heart is with the Celestial Mountains
My body now ageing by the water.

These poems were written by the poet late in life, during his years of seclusion, expressing his regret that he had already grown old while his noble ambitions had yet to be fulfilled.

Lu You and Tang Wan

After their marriage, Lu You and Tang Wan got along very well with each other. However, Lu's mother kept finding fault with Tang Wan and eventually forced them to divorce.

Ten years later, Lu You happened to run into Tang Wan with her second husband while visiting the Shen Garden.

Tang Wan sent him a meal.

She hasn't forgotten me!

After a drink, he came back to the Shen Garden tipsy, and wrote a poem on the wall set to the tune of 'Hairpin Phoenix'.

Pink hands, yellow wine.
Spring in the city, willows verdant over the palace-wall.
Cold is the east wind,
Joys so fragile,
Heart filled with sorrow,
And years of separation.
Wrong, wrong and wrong.

Spring as usual, yet we are hollow and thin.
Tear tracks, red eyes, the handkerchief wet through.
Peach blossoms fallen,
Pools and pavilions deserted.
Our oath still remains,
Too much for a silk letter.
No, no and no.

Lu You revisited the Garden when he turned 68. Tang Wan was already dead by then. Rereading his poem on the wall he could not hold back his tears.

Dreams dashed, my love lost 40 years, old willows with no more catkins dancing…

The story of the moving love and tragic marriage of Lu You and Tang Wan as told in the poems have since been adapted by various playrights and remains popular even today.

Xin Qiji (1140–1207)

Xin Qiji was an army general. When he was 22, Xin gathered an army of 2,000 men and joined the uprising led by Geng Jing to combat the Jin invaders advancing southwards. He later served the Southern Song regime and gained outstanding achievements at his post. Eager to recover the central plains, Xin submitted many memorials, but as the Southern Song regime was content to retain sovereignty over a part of the country, his dream remained unrealised.

Thoughts on Climbing Beigu Pavilion at Jingkou

Where can I see the Central Plains?
A perfect vantage point offered at Beigu Pavilion.
Stories of dynastic rises and falls abound since days of yore,
Going on still,
Like the rolling Yangtze River.
Leading a legion of helmeted men, the young king Sun Quan
Defended the southeast through repeated battles.
Who could match him of all heroes then?
Only Cao Cao and Liu Bei.
Would that I had a son like Sun!

Bold and unconstrained, this poem calls on heroes to recover the central plains through a memorial description of Sun Quan, ruler of the State of Wu during the Three Kingdoms period.

Tune: An Ugly Girl

Litle did I know of sorrow in my youth.
Yet I loved to climb towers.
I climbed towers
And sought to express sorrow in poems.

This is one of Xin Qiji's most popular poems. A vivid and compelling description of how youths understand sorrow differently from the middle-aged, it can easily strike a chord among readers.

Using *Ci* to Condemn Evil Persons

Xin Qiji was born in Northern China, which was occupied by the Jin army. One day, when he was 10, guests came to visit the Xins. Among the guests was a Jin officer.

Xin's grandfather asked Xin Qiji to perform swordplay for the guests.

I'll kill all the evil Jin people some day in the future and recover the central plains.

Once, a teacher asked Xin Qiji and his classmates about their ambitions.

What are you going to do when you grow up?

Be a high-ranking official!

I don't want to take any official post! I'll condemn all evil persons in the world with my poems and kill all the Jin devils with my sword.

When he grew up, Xin Qiji joined the volunteer army to resist the Jin invaders. Meanwhile, he also composed a large number of poems and essays full of fighting spirit. To some extent his childhood wish was fulfilled.

Wen Tianxiang (1236–1283)

Wen Tianxiang was the last prime minister of the Southern Song Dynasty. The Mongols established the Yuan Dynasty following its conquest of the Jin Dynasty and advanced south to wipe out the Southern Song regime. Wen Tianxiang attempted to negotiate peace with the Yuan army on behalf of Southern Song and was arrested, but managed to escape and organised an army of volunteers to try to recover the lost territories.

Eventually, his army was defeated and he was captured and imprisoned in Dadu (Beijing). He refused to serve the Yuan empire and was finally executed.

Crossing the Lonely Sea

My eventful career started with academic honor,
Arms flashed and flames raged in every corner.
The country falling apart and catkins in wind dancing,
My life rose and fell as duckweeds in rain floating.
Speaking of Terror on the Terror Beach,
Uttering a lonely sigh on the Lonely Sea.
Who, of all men since olden days, can live forever?
A loyal heart left behind will shine forever in historical records.

Demonstrating an indomitable and undaunted spirit, the last two lines are widely quoted.

Ode to the Noble Spirit

Betwixt heaven and earth exists a noble spirit,
Giving shapes to myriad things in the world.
Below, it molds the rivers and mountains,
And above, it fashions the sun and stars.
Man it informs with a righteous spirit,
So thick and profuse, it fills up the vast sky.
In times of national peace and stability,
This spirit is seen in an honest government;
In times of crisis it is manifested in men of integrity,
And their names will go down in history.

The poet lists many historical personalities known for their lofty ideals and noble deeds to illustrate the noble spirit.

Preferring Death to Surrender

During the closing years of the Southern Song Dynasty, the Yuan army launched a full-scale attack on the capital city of Lin-an. Wen donated all his family properties and organised a legion to defend the country.

The emperor of the Southern Song regime appointed Wen prime minister and dispatched him to negotiate with the Yuan army.

You must all surrender, or none of you will live.

Boyan, prime minister of the Yuan empire.

I am a subject of the Song empire. I would rather die than surrender.

So, Boyan put Wen under house arrest.

Wen was captured again. Emperor Shizu of the Yuan Dynasty came in person to persuade him to submit.

If you serve me, I'll appoint you prime minister.

I am content to serve Song as its minister. I have no wish to serve you.

Then, what do you want to do now?

Die for my country.

Wen was executed in 1283.

Later, Wen managed to escape and went back to the South where he continued to lead the war of resistence against the Yuan army.

LI QINGZHAO — CHINA'S MOST CELEBRATED *CI* POETESS

Li Qingzhao (1084–1155)

There appeared a prominent *Ci* poetess named Li Qingzhao during the Southern Song Dynasty. Written in an elegant, subtle and soul-stirring style, her poems dwell on sentiments over separation and the changing social situation. She is recognised as the greatest *Ci* poetess in Chinese literature.

A Famous *Ci* by Li Qingzhao

Tune: Sounds Long and Slow

I seek and search,
Lonely and cold,
Forlorn, depressed and sad.
Now spring is giving way to winter,
It is a time most difficult to keep fit.
How can two or three cups of light wine,
Hold back the evening blasts?
Wild geese flying overhead,
I, deep in sorrow,
Have seen them before.
Withered blossoms collect on the ground,
Wilting and decaying,
Who would come and pick them?
Standing by the sill alone,
How come it turns dark unawares?
Phoenix trees in a drizzle,
Raindrops still dripping at dusk.
These scenes,
Cannot be grasped with a word—sorrow.

The poem expresses the loneliness she felt in the sunset of her life.

A Sprig of Plum

The scent of pink lotus roots fades and the jade mat feels autumn.
With my robe slightly loosened,
I board alone the orchid boat.
Whose silk mail is it coming from the sky?
A time when wild geese fly back in a
formation,
Moonlight floods the western chamber.
Petals fall just as water flows by itself.
One yearning
Links two persons in sorrow.
No way to overcome this sentiment,
First it appears on my brow,
And then rushes into my heart.

Here in this poem, Li Qingzhao
expressed her yearning for her husband
after their separation.

A Short Poem Composed in Summer

I shall be a hero when I'm alive,
Or a chief ghost when I'm gone.
I'm still thinking of Xiang Yu,
Who refused to cross the river.

Li Qingzhao was also a patriot who had
suffered personally after the collapse of the
Northern Song Dynasty. She was disgusted with
the Southern Song regime which was
content to remain in the safety of the
south. This poem is an attack by innuendo
on the incompetent Southern
Song government through a
eulogy of Xiang Yu who
preferred to die rather than live
in disgrace.

A Story of Li Qingzhao

Li Qingzhao's father was Li Gefei, a notable disciple of the eminent writer Su Shi. Her mother was also a good essay writer. Thanks to this excellent domestic environment, she was very well-versed in Chinese classics, history and literature.

At 18 she was married to Zhao Mingcheng. Their common pursuits and interests ensured a happy conjugal life.

Zhao Mingcheng liked to collect ancient inscriptions on metals and stones. Being poor, they used to pledge their clothes at pawnshops for money to collect tablets. The couple would eat fruits while appreciating the inscriptions together.

Later, Zhao Mingcheng was assigned a post in Qingzhou. Li Qingzhao wrote the poem, 'Drunk among Blossoms' and sent it to him. Deeply moved, Zhao read it over and over.

He spent three days and nights composing 15 poems in reply to his wife.

He scattered lines from Li Qingzhao's poem in his own and asked his friend Lu Defu for his opinion.

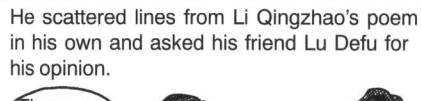

There are only three good lines in this group of poems.

Which lines?

Don't tell me not to sorrow, Curtains in the west wind, I am thinner than chrysanthemums.

Haha! These are Qingzhao's lines.

Later, as the Jin army advanced south, a huge number of their collections, which filled more than 10 rooms, were destroyed by the flames of war.

Zhao Mingcheng later died of illness. Grieving, Li Qingzhao fell seriously ill. Afterwards, she led a poor and wandering life. It is said that she later remarried a man of poor character, but the marriage did not last.

Having lost her home and family, Li Qingzhao decided to go on a boat tour when spring came.

I only fear the light boat on Shuangxi stream, Cannot bear the weight of so much sorrow.

SONG DYNASTY *HUA-BEN* (STORYTELLERS' SCRIPTS)

During the Song Dynasty, towns and cities prospered, and a flourishing popular culture developed. The art of story-telling was extremely popular then. Storytellers based their stories on scripts, which became the forerunners of vernacular Chinese fiction.

To appeal to the audience, these scripts focused on clear and lively plot development. In addition, colloquial diction was widely adopted, setting this new fictional form apart from the classical-language tales of the Tang Dynasty.

Song Dynasty *hua-ben* fall into four categories, among which the most important are "short talks," which are short and aim to mirror current social conditions; and "historical talks" (also known as "popular talks"), which are based on history. Being longer, "historical talks" are divided into continuing episodes.

A popular Song Dynasty *hua-ben*:

The Wrongful Execution of Cui Ning

What are you doing there?

Liu Gui struggled with the ruffian and was killed with a hatchet.

Wang Jr. got up early next morning and set out for home. She met a young man named Cui Ning along the way.

Since we're going the same way, let's travel together.

Wang Jr, Liu Gui was murdered. You must go back for a cross-examination.

You killed your husband and ran away with his money!

You've even seduced a man!

Fifteen strings of cash! Here are the spoils! You cannot deny it!

I earned this money by selling silks in the town.

Nobody believed them. So Wang Jr. and Cui Ning were delivered to the local magistrate.

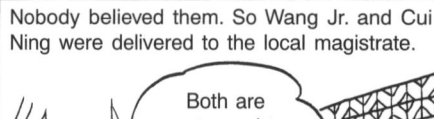

Both are sentenced to execution for murder!

A year later, Wang Sr. was captured by Chief Jingshan of a group of mountain robbers and forced to become his wife.

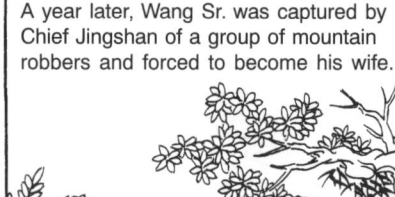

One day, the chief told her:

You know, I once killed a man, but luckily, I had two scapegoats. Ha ha!

After asking him for more details, Wang Sr. realized that this man was the true culprit.

So she reported the case to the local government and the chief robber was brought to justice.

Cui Ning and Wang Jr were finally vindicated. This story exposed the careless way local authorities handled cases and punished people.

LITERATURE OF THE YUAN DYNASTY

Genghis Khan founded the Mongol Empire in 1206, and it was designated as the Yuan Dynasty by Kublai Khan in 1271. The Southern Song regime was eliminated in 1279. During the Yuan Dynasty, despite serious ethnic prejudices, the weakening of the long-dominant Confucian ideology resulted in a rather lively literary scene. The unique poetic form of *san-qu* (literally, separate or dispersed songs) developed during this period, and the fields of fiction and drama also flourished.

SAN-QU

San-qu appeared at a time when the *Ci* poetic form of the Song Dynasty placed overemphasis on elegance. It originated from popular music and songs.

Fresh and lively, *san-qu* makes extensive use of colloquial language and is thus very suitable for singing. *San-qu* is often included in *za-ju* (a dramatic form popular during the Yuan Dynasty) as arias, or it may also stand alone as a lyrical poetic form, hence the term *san-qu*. It has two forms: *xiao-ling* and *tao-shu*. *Xiao-ling* refers to single songs and *tao-shu* refers to sets of sequential lyrics based on at least two tunes.

Ma Zhiyuan (ca. 1250–1324)

Ma Zhiyuan is a representative and outstanding writer of *san-qu*. At the same time, his *za-ju* plays are also universally recognised.

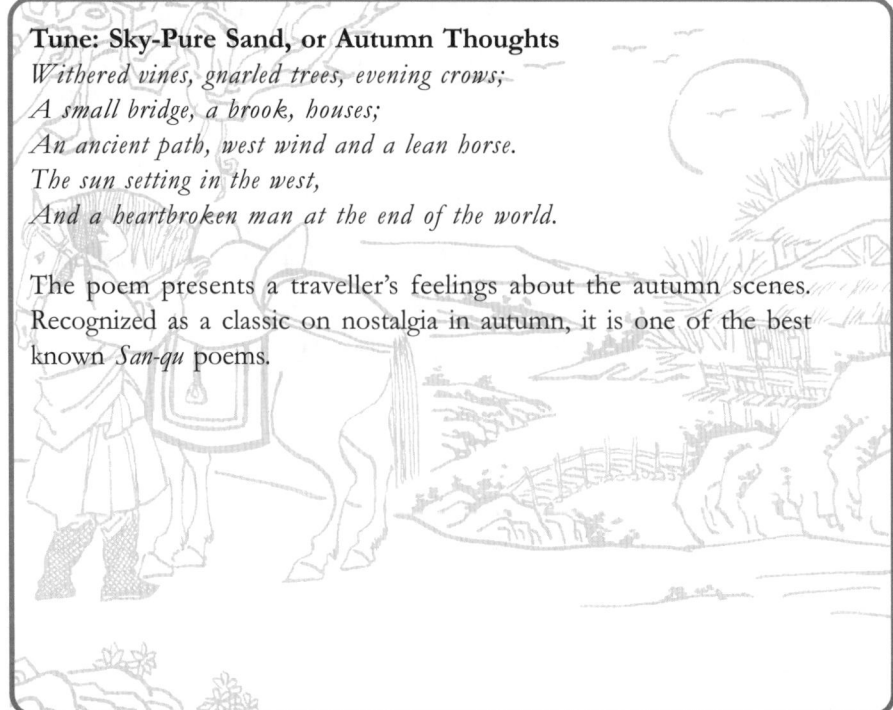

Tune: Sky-Pure Sand, or Autumn Thoughts
Withered vines, gnarled trees, evening crows;
A small bridge, a brook, houses;
An ancient path, west wind and a lean horse.
The sun setting in the west,
And a heartbroken man at the end of the world.

The poem presents a traveller's feelings about the autumn scenes. Recognized as a classic on nostalgia in autumn, it is one of the best known *San-qu* poems.

Zhang Yanghao (1270–1329)

Here we have another immortal *san-qu*.

Tune: Sheep on the Mountain Slope
Peaks gathering, waves seething,
Path to Tong Pass lined with mountains and rivers.
Looking to the West Capital, I feel distressed.
Saddened to see, where Qin and Han dynasties ruled,
Thousands of palaces reduced to dust.
Dynasties rise, common folks suffer.
Dynasties fall, common folks also suffer.

The poem starts with a description of the majestic scenes the poet saw on his way to Tong Pass. Looking ahead to Xi'an, he could not help thinking of the rise and fall of dynasties, and concluded with a sigh that common folks always suffer whether a dynasty rises or falls. A perfect unity is achieved here of art and thought in this *xiao-ling*, which ensures its enduring popularity.

Guan Hanqing (ca. 1220–1300)

Best known as a *za-ju* playwright (see p.111 for details), Guan Hanqing also wrote *san-qu*. He is an expert in depicting the romantic relationships between men and women, as can be seen in the lively exchange below.

Tune: Just A Half
Quiet and deserted outside the green-gauze window,
Kneeling at the bedside, he wants to make love to me.
"Faithless," I scold and turn away.
Though my words sound angry,
I am actually half refusing and half willing.

Sui Jingchen (dates of birth and death not available)

Of all the *san-qu* works in the Yuan Dynasty, Sui Jingchen's 'Tune: *Ban She (Shao bian)* — Emperor Gaozu's Homecoming', stands out as the best-known. The piece narrates in a satiric vein Liu Bang's grand homecoming following his ascent to the royal throne. To Liu's surprise, a villager runs up to him and lists all the misdeeds he committed in the past: "You were no good when you lived here; you changed a contract to gain profit; to repay wine debts, you stole several bushels of beans… the money you owe me…the grain you owe me… I knew you as Liu the Third, on what grounds did you change your name to Han Gaozu?"

ZA-JU

Za-ju is another new literary genre that rose to prominence in the Yuan Dynasty. *San-qu* and *za-ju* are jointly designated as *yuan-qu* by historians of Chinese literature.

Za-ju are stage plays. Structurally, a *za-ju* is generally divided into four acts corresponding to exposition, development, climax and denouement. Sometimes the script includes an additional part called a "wedge", which connects the different acts. The roles have singing, speaking and action parts. Lyrics are the focus of *za-ju* scripts.

In each act, there is only one lead singer, while all other characters engage in speaking or actions. Besides the male and female leads, typical characters in a *za-ju* include *jing* (painted faces/clown or villain), *gu* (ennuchs), *bu'er* (old women), *lai'er* (children), *bei lao* (old men) and other roles.

Guan Hanqing (ca. 1220–1300)

Considered the greatest *za-ju* playwright, Guan Hanqing's status is similar to Shakespeare's in the West. Altogether, he wrote over 60 *za-ju* plays, and his masterpiece is *The Injustice Done to Dou E*. Not only did Guan Hanqing write scripts, he sometimes also played a singing role on the stage.

At that time, a *za-ju* playwright did not enjoy a respected social status. Some people mocked at his performance. To this, he responded with witty tunes to dismiss his critics and show his deep commitment to *za-ju*.

> *I am a tinkling pea of copper. You cannot destroy me through steaming, boiling, trampling or baking... Even if you remove my teeth, wrench my mouth, cripple my legs, cut off my hands, or Heaven inflicts all kinds of diseases on me, I won't give up...*

Wang Shifu (1295–1307)

The Romance of West Chamber by Wang Shifu is internationally renowned. Characters in the play such as Hong-niang, Cui Yingying and Scholar Zhang are now household names. With no interest in fame or wealth, Wang Shifu lived in poverty, residing in a thatched house and wearing coarse clothes. Nevertheless, he had his own way of enjoying life, drinking wine, reciting poems and touring mountains and rivers.

Wang Shifu Breaks a Stone Table Writing *The Romance of West Chamber*

Wang Shifu used to write scripts at a stone table outside his house. Whenever he finished a section, he would read it aloud while rapping the table with an iron paperweight. After several years, the flat table surface had become uneven and a corner was even chipped.

The Injustice Done to Dou E

by *Guan Hanqing.*

Dou Tianzhang, a poor scholar, borrowed some money from Mistress Cai. However, he could not repay the debt.

Mistress Cai, I'd like to pledge my daughter Dou E to you as a future bride for your son.

It was not long before Mistress Cai's son died and so Dou E became a widow.

Zhang Lü'er, a ruffian, had designs on Dou E.

What a pity you're widowed at such a young age! Why not come and live with me?

Behave yourself!

It will be easy to get Dou E when Mistress Cai dies from poison.

When Mistress Cai fell ill, Zhang Lü'er obtained some poison.

Zhang Lü'er put some poison in the sheep-gut soup Dou E cooked for her mother-in-law. But Zhang's father drank the soup by mistake and died instead.

Zhang Lü'er brought a false charge against Dou E, claiming that she had killed his father.

Dou E, you put poison in the soup!

No, I didn't!

Zhang Lü'er bribed the magistrate and Dou E was sentenced to death.

Before her execution, Dou E uttered three curses.

If I am innocent, after my head is cut off, let my hot blood spill onto this white cloth; let heavy snow fall on this June day and cover my body; and let there be a three-year drought in Chu-Zhou!

Her words came true. A heavy snow fell and proved her innocence.

A few years later, Dou E's father returned as an official and vindicated his daughter.

My poor daughter, your name has been cleared at last. Rest in peace.

The Romance of West Chamber

by *Wang Shifu.*

Scholar Zhang Gong was preparing for the Imperial Examination at Pujiu Temple when he met Cui Yingying, daughter of Prime Minister Cui. They fell in love at first sight

Surrender Cui Yingying to us!

At the time, Sun Feihu, leader of a mutiny, ordered a siege of the temple.

I shall bethroth my daughter to anyone who can repulse the army!

I know White-Steed General Du Que. I'll write a letter to him and ask him to drive away the mutineers.

The general sent some troops and raised the siege.

Zhang is only a poor scholar, unworthy of my daughter. We might as well just let them be brother and sister.

Hong-niang, a maidservant of Yingying, sympathised with them very much.

Please let me be your go-between, Mistress!

With her help, Scholar Zhang and Cui Yingying met at West Chamber on a moonlit night.

They were discovered by Madam Cui.

Tomorrow, you will go to Chang'an for the Imperial Exam. If you fail, I won't allow Yingying to marry you.

Yingying saw Scholar Zhang off at a roadside hut.

Please come back as soon as possible.

Please rest assured. I'll come back to you with the title of No.1 Scholar.

Scholar Zhang passed the examination with great honour and returned to marry Yingying. So the two lovers got together in the end.

Autumn in the Han Palace by Ma Zhiyuan

There are many other well-known *za-ju* plays. Ma Zhiyuan's history play *Autumn in the Han Palace* tells the story of Wang Zhaojun's marriage to the Hun chief controlling northern China at the time and praises her nobility in sacrificing herself for her country. The play arrived in Europe through an English translation in 1829.

The Zhao Family Orphan by Ji Junxiang

The play tells a story that occurred during the Spring and Autumn Period. Zhao Dun was murdered by his political rival and his whole family was also on the brink of being exterminated. Cheng Ying, a retainer of the family, rescued Zhao Dun's grandson by substituting him with his own son. The orphan grew up and avenged his family. Brought to Europe in the 18th century, the play was staged in the Paris Royal Theatre once.

Southern Drama

Dramatic art also developed in the southern part of China during the Yuan Dynasty. There are five famous plays of this type:

The Story of the Lute has been called "the divine work among all old tales, and the acme of dramatic art". It tells the story of Zhao Wu-niang's search for her husband and showcases her filial piety and virtue.

Praying to the Moon is a story of true love played out during the chaotic time of war.

The Story of the Hairpin is a story about a couple's struggles against some high-ranking officials.

The Story of White Hare relates how Li San-niang was reunited with her husband after going through a series of trials. The heroine is depicted vividly as a steadfast and faithful figure.

Killing Dogs tells how Yang Yuezhen finds a way to reconcile her husband Sun Hua with her brother-in-law Sun Rong. Yang Yuezhen is portrayed as a model wife.

LITERATURE OF THE MING DYNASTY

During the Ming dynasty, fiction, drama and other genres of popular literature flourished and many great works were accomplished. In fiction, there appeared such classics as *Journey to the West, Golden Lotus, Canonisation of the Gods, Stories to Enlighten Men, Stories to Warn Men, Stories to Awaken Men, Amazing Stories I* and *Amazing Stories II*.

ROMANCE OF THE THREE KINGDOMS

Author: Luo Guanzhong (years of birth and death unknown). Only scant records exist today about him.

Origin: *The Romance of Three Kingdoms* appeared in the late Yuan Dynasty. The official history of the Three Kingdoms was recorded by Chen Shou in *Records of the Three Kingdoms* as early as the Jin Dynasty. Stories about the period also circulated among the people. *The Romance of Three Kingdoms* is based on a combination of the outline of Chen Shou's *Records*, unofficial historical accounts and folktales of different periods. Thus, it is a book of which "seventy percent is true to history and thirty percent made up."

Content: The novel narrates how, during the late Eastern Han Dynasty, Cao Cao, Liu Bei and Sun Quan ultimately carved up China into three parts. A wide range of characters are vividly depicted in the novel and many episodes in the novel have become household stories, such as "Liu Bei, Guan Yu and Zhang Fei Become Sworn Brothers in the Peach Garden", "Liu Bei Pays Three Visits to the Thatched House where Zhuge Liang Lives" and "Zhuge Liang Vexes Zhou Yu Three Times". Stories of the Three Kingdoms are known across the world, and the spirit of loyalty they extol has grown into an important part of the Chinese cultural heritage.

Three Sworn Brothers in the Peach Garden

from *The Romance of Three Kingdoms.*

During the late Easterm Han Dynasty, the government was corrupt and thoughts turned to rebellion across the land. Zhang Jiao organised a rebel army called the Yellow Scarves. Liu Yan, prefect of Youzhou, quickly called for warriors to fight the rebels.

Alas!

A true man should serve his country. Why do you sigh?

I am Liu Bei, descended from the imperial family. I wish to fight the rebels and aid the people, but my power is limited.

My name is Zhang Fei. I have resources to outfit some local soldiers. Let's do something great together!

Then the two ran into Guan Yu, who had come to answer the call for warriors.

I killed a noble who used his position to bully people, so I'm now wandering to avoid the authorities. I heard that there is a mobilisation here. So I came to enlist.

So, the three men went into a peach garden. There they made offerings to Heaven and Earth and became sworn brothers, swearing to join hands to serve the country and protect the people.

Paying Three Visits to the Thatched House

from *The Romance of Three Kingdoms.*

When Liu Bei's strategist Xu Shu left, he recommended Zhuge Liang to him.

Zhuge Liang is a man of extraordinary genius!

When will he return?

Liu Bei, Guan Yu and Zhang Fei went to call on Zhuge Liang, but he was out.

I'm not sure. It might be three to five days, or ten days.

Zhuge Liang was not at home either during their second visit. They only met his younger brother and father-in-law.

They did not see Zhuge Liang until their third visit.

Seeing Liu Bei's sincerity, Zhuge Liang agreed to help. Later, with his assistance, Liu Bei founded the Kingdom of Shu, which, together with Wei and Wu, became the three powers that dominated China during that period.

WATER MARGIN

Author: Shi Nai'an (ca. 1296–1370). Born into a poor family, Shi only started school when he was 19, but passed the county-level Imperial Examination at 20 and the provincial-level examination at 30. He served as an official at Qiantang for some time before retiring to his hometown to work on *Water Margin*.

Origin: *Water Margin* is based on the uprising led by Song Jiang during the late Northern Song dynasty. Legends about the uprising had already started to appear in *hua-ben* during the Southern Song Dynasty and *za-ju* plays during the Yuan Dynasty. Besides drawing extensively on these materials, Shi Nai'an also put in his own creative efforts when writing the novel. The earliest edition of the novel comprised 100 chapters, while a later edition comprised 102 chapters. Later, Jin Shengtan, a distinguished literary scholar who lived during the period of transition from the Ming Dynasty to the Qing Dynasty, revised the work, retaining only the first 70 chapters and adding a prologue.

Content: The novel describes how 108 heroes, including Song Jiang, Lin Chong, Wu Song and Lu Zhishen, were compelled to revolt by corrupt officials and local tyrants who committed all kinds of crimes, showing the determination of the people to fight against darkness and corruption. *"bi shang liang shan (*driven to Mount Liang)" has become an idiom in Chinese to mean a situation where people are driven into a corner and have no choice but to rebel.

Wu Song Kills a Tiger and his Sister-in-Law

from *Water Margin.*

Wu Song was travelling to Qinghe County to see his elder brother Wu the Elder. He stopped at a tavern in Yanggu County for a drink before crossing Jingyang Ridge.

Sir, people usually get drunk after drinking three bowls of wine in our tavern. But you have drunk 18 bowls!

Also, there is a fierce tiger on this ridge attacking people. You'd better stay until tomorrow and cross with other people.

Wu Song would not listen and went up the ridge, where he ran into the tiger.

After a fierce struggle, Wu Song killed the beast with his fists.

What a tiger-killing hero!

Seeing this, a group of local hunters admired him very much.

Thus, he was employed as a constable in Yanggu County.

Wu Song met his brother Wu the Elder in the street and went home with him.

Wu the Elder had married Pan Jinlian, a pretty maid of a rich family. As many dissolute idlers came to pester Pan from time to time, Wu the Elder moved to Yanggu County.

Brother, why not come and live with us?

Sister-in-law.

Impressed by Wu Song, Pan Jinlian fell in love with him and tried to seduce him.

Brother, please finish the remaining wine in the cup if you have any feeling for me.

After Wu Song left his brother's home angrily, the magistrate of Yanggu County sent him away on a mission.

With the aid of her neighbor, Mistress Wang, Pan Jinlian seduced Ximen Qing, a wealthy and powerful man.

Wu the Elder caught the two adulterers and was wounded by Ximen Qing.

At the instigation of Mistress Wang, Pan Jinlian poisoned Wu the Elder.

To cover up the evidence, Mistress Wang, Pan Jinlian and Ximen Qing had Wu the Elder's body cremated.

When Wu Song came back, he became suspicious of the death of his brother and uncovered the truth through investigation.

In front of his neighbours, Wu Song forced Mistress Wang and Pan Jinlian to tell the truth, took down what they said and then killed Pan Jinlian.

Wu Song lodged a suit. However, the magistrate had been bribed and dismissed his case.

Afterwards he also killed Ximen Qing and surrendered himself to the court with two heads, affidavits and Mistress Wang.

Having high regard for Wu Song's upright character, the official hearing his case decided to only banish him, and sentenced Mistress Wang to death.

JOURNEY TO THE WEST

Author: From childhood, Wu Cheng'en (1500–1582) read widely and partiuclarly enjoyed collecting legends and anecdotes told among the ordinary people. He served as an official for some time and then quit the post. Returning to his hometown, he indulged in poems and wine. It is said that some of his friends and townsmen, having obtained high-ranking official posts, often continued to seek his help in writing memorials to the emperor.

Origin: *Journey to the West* is a mythological novel based on the true story of a Tang Dynasty monk, Xuanzang (602–664). He spent 18 years travelling to India to study Buddhism and returned to China with 657 volumes of Buddhist scriptures written in Sanskrit. His disciples compiled *Records of the Western Regions during the Great Tang Dynasty* (dictated by Xuanzang and recorded and edited by his disciples) and *Life of the Tripitaka Master of the Great Ci'en Temple* as a record of Xuanzang's experiences. Later, more and more fantastic details were added to his story in folktales. Wu Cheng'en wrote his outstanding mythological novel based on these stories.

Content: Wu Cheng'en invented three distinctive nonhuman disciples for Xuanzang (Tripitaka) — the untamable Monkey King Sun Wukong, the lazy and gluttonous Pigsy and the sedate and silent Sandy. The Monkey, who is capable of 72 transformations and other magic skills, is extremely popular among readers of different age groups. The fiction narrates the 81 calamities and confrontations they go through. Many episodes are very well written, such as "Su Wukong Creates Havoc in Heaven," "Smashing the Corpse Fiend Three Times", "Crossing the Fiery Mountain", "True and False Su Wukong" and "A Kingdom of Women".

Sun Wukong Smashes the
Corpse Fiend Three Times

This mountain looks sinister. It may be haunted by evil spirits.

Escorting Monk Xuanzang on his journey to the West for Buddhist scriptures, Su Wukong, Piggy and Sandy came to a dangerous place in the mountain.

Wukong, go and get some food for us.

After Sun Wukong left, the corpse fiend wanted to take this opportunity to get Xuanzang.

Ok, Master, I will go and pick some peaches.

It was said that eating his flesh would make one immortal. So the fiend transformed itself into a girl.

Mactor, I have brought some food for you.

OTHER NOVELS

Golden Lotus

Written by Lan Ling Xiao Xiao Sheng, *Golden Lotus* is the first full-length novel written independently by a man of letters. It is also the first novel describing human relationships, social affairs and family life. The novel revolves around the lascivious Ximen Qing and his three concubines—Pan Jinlian, Li Ping'er and Chun Mei. The title of the novel actually consists of the names of these three female characters.

Canonisation of the Gods

Written by Xu Zhonglin, *Canonisation of the Gods* is a fantastic account of gods and monsters. It tells how Jiang Ziya helped Emperor Wu of Zhou launch a crusade against Emperor Zhou of Shang. The novel portrays many gods and monsters with various magic weapons and powers, such as clairvoyance, clairaudience, and the ability to fly or dive into the ground.

THREE COLLECTIONS OF STORIES ABOUT MEN AND TWO SERIES OF AMAZING STORIES

Feng Menglong (1574–1646)

The Ming Dynasty was also a period when short stories flourished, and Feng Menglong was the paramount short story writer of that time. Highly erudite, he was well-versed in poetry, *Ci*, songs, rhymed prose, historiography, fiction, drama and the fine arts. Unfortunately, he suffered repeated setbacks in his career and was not granted the scholarly title of *Gongsheng* (a student allowed to study at the Imperial College) until he turned 57, to fill a vacancy. Following the collapse of the Ming Dynasty, he engaged actively in the struggle against the Qing regime.

Feng Menglong wrote and compiled three collections of short stories: *Stories to Enlighten Men*, *Stories to Warn Men* and *Stories to Awaken Men*. Comprising 120 tales, they feature a wide range of subject matters such as love and the many aspects of society.

Ling Mengchu (1580–1644)

Ling Mengchu was another prominent short-story writer active in the literary scene of the Ming Dynasty besides Feng Menglong. He wrote and compiled two collections of short stories: *Amazing Stories First Series* and *Amazing Stories Second Series* based on unofficial historical notes, previous fictional works and anecdotes. Some stories reflect the social conditions during the late Ming period while others feature unwholesome or superstitious content.

Du Shi-niang Angrily Sinks Her Jewel Chest

by *Feng Menglong.*

DRAMA

Many great dramatic works were also produced during the Ming Dynasty, and Tang Xianzu (1550–1616) was the foremost playwright of that period. His four plays — *The Purple Hairpin*, *The Peony Pavilion*, *The Tale of Nanke* and *The Tale of Handan* are collectively termed "Four Dreams of Linchuan". The reason is that Tang Xianzu was a native of Linchuan in Jiangxi Province, and these four plays all share the theme of dreams. *The Peony Pavilion* stands out among all his plays and even enjoys a high international reputation. When assessing the artistic merits of *The Peony Pavilion*, a critic once remarked: "the appearance of *The Peony Pavilion* has devalued *The Romance of West Chamber*."

The Peony Pavilion
by *Tang Xianzu.*

POETRY AND PROSE

The Former Seven Masters are a group of writers who were active in the mid-Ming Dynasty. They are Li Mengyang, He Jingming, Kang Hai, Wang Jiusi, Bian Gong, Wang Tingxiang and Xu Zhenqing. They maintained that Ming poetry should be modelled on High Tang poetry, classical-style poetry should follow the style of the Wei Dynasty, and prose writers should learn from the writers of the Qin and Han Dynasties. The literary campaign they launched was called the Classical Revival Movement.

> **A Song of Reply, by Li Mengyang**
> *Long is the beauty's silk belt,*
> *Blown by wind, it touches not the ground.*
> *Bending to pick up a jade hairpin,*
> *Another from her hair falling.*

The Tang and Song School appeared during the reign of Emperor Jiajing in the mid-Ming period, and members include Wang Shenzhong, Tang Shunzhi, Mao Kun and Gui Youguang. Though holding up Tang poetry as its model, the school in fact attached more importance to Song Dynasty Neo-Confucianism.

Gui Youguang (1507–1571) is the most accomplished prose writer of the Tang and Song school, and is known for writing of familial love in a plain style. His representative works include "A Note on Xiangji Study", "A Few Words on My Late Mother" and "A Note on Burying Cold Blossoms".

The Later Seven Masters were associated in the 27th year of Emperor Jiajing's reign (1548). They were headed by Li Panlong. While they challenged the Neo-Confucian tenets of the Tang and Song School, they fully accepted the beliefs of the Former Seven Masters, placing great emphasis on modelling their writings on classical styles. Thus, their literary productions were seriously restricted. The group consists of Li Panlong, Wang Shizhen, Xu Zhongxing, Liang Youyu, Zong Chen, Xie Zhen and Wu Guolun.

A Border Song — Seeing Off Yuan Mei, by Li Panlong
White feathers like frost went out of the pass in the cold,
Messages of Tartars invading reached Chang'an.
The moon from the west mountain shining on watch towers,
How many soldiers can see it on horseback?

The first two lines of this poem illustrate the urgent messages of attack, while the latter half vividly depicts the night scene and the love the soldiers felt for their city.

Gong'an School
Yuan Hongdao (1568–1610) and his two brothers, elder brother Yuan Zongdao and younger brother Yuan Zhongdao, constituted the core members of the Gong'an School. The school owed its name to their hometown, Gong'an county of Hubei Province. One quality the three brothers had in common was their realistic depictions of scenes and individual native feelings. They are also called the "School of Native Feeling".

Jingling School

After the Gong'an School emerged the Jingling School, represented by Zhong Xing and Tan Yuanchun. While subscribing to the motto of the Gong'an School "Express the Native Feelings", the school also advocated "originality and innovation." Such literary perspectives were quite popular during the period of transition from the Ming Dynasty to the Qing Dynasty.

Xu Wei (1521–1593)

Xu Wei was an unfettered scholar known for his outstanding achievements in painting, calligraphy and poetry. His poetry was highly appreciated by Yuan Hongdao. He was also a noted strategist and worked for Viceroy Hu Zongxian as a staff member and participated in the war against the invading *Wuokou* (Japanese pirates).

> **A Triumphant Song at Mount Kan**
> *Crossed at dusk are daggers and lances,*
> *Blood onto men cold wind blows.*
> *At dawn are seen mounted soldiers returning,*
> *Red ice on chill armours hanging.*

Qi Jiguang (1528–1587)

Qi Jiguang is known both as a poet and as a general who led the combat against the invading *Wuokou*. His poems are is filled with lofty sentiments.

> **Composed on Horseback**
> *Galloping from south to north for His Majesty,*
> *Smiling by flowering rivers and at moonlit borders.*
> *Three hundred and sixty days throughout a year,*
> *Are spent mostly on horseback with dagger-axe in hand.*

Xia Wanchun (1631–1647)

Following the fall of the Ming Dynasty, there appeared a group of poets supporting the anti-Manchu struggle . Xia Wanchun is one such poet. His father Xia Yunyi and his mentor Chen Zilong are both anti-Manchu heroes. In 1644, the rebel forces led by Li Zicheng took over Beijing. Xia wrote letters to 40 squires in his hometown, persuading them to provide financial support for a campaign to restore the Ming emperor to the throne. At the news that the Manchu army had crossed the Shanhai Pass, he participated actively in the battles against the alien invaders. When he was captured, the notorious traitor Hong Chengchou came and tried to talk him into surrendering but was firmly rejected. He was only 17 years old when he was executed. His poems brim over with a heroic spirit.

Adieu to My Hometown

Three years I have tramped like a guest,
Unfortunately today my hands are bound.
The endless land is filled with tears,
Who says that broad is sky and ground?
Knowing that death is coming nigh,
To part with my hometown is so hard.
The day when my defiant ghost returns,
Banners of struggle flap still in the sky.

LITERATURE OF THE QING DYNASTY

The Qing Dynasty was a golden age for novels and short stories, mainly independent works by men of letters, with close attention to realistic depiction of everyday life and development of fictional form. The most outstanding example is *The Dream of the Red Chamber*. Another seminal work is the short story collection, *Strange Stories from a Chinese* Studio.

STRANGE STORIES FROM A CHINESE STUDIO

Author: Born into a literary family, Pu Songling (1640–1715) had a keen interest in the Imperial Examination from childhood and passed the exams at three levels including the county and prefecture with top honors at 19. However, he repeatedly failed in subsequent higher-level exams, and it was only at the age of 71 that he acquired the title of *Gongsheng*, a student allowed to study in the Imperial College. He spent most of his life in his hometown as a private tutor except for a one-year appointment as a magistrate aide at Baoying County of Jiangsu Province. He had suffered greatly from the system of the imperial civil service examination in spite of his talent. It is no wonder that he often exposed the defects in the examination system in his writings.

Content: Pu Songling's *Strange Stories* is considered the most successful and influential collection of short stories in classical Chinese literature. Consisting of nearly five hundred stories, the collection is partially drawn from folklore, partially from the author's creative imagination. Pu Songling used the strange world of ghosts, goblins, fox-fairies and flower spirits to satirise the social conditions of his time and human nature, while extolling love. Love stories constitute the bulk of the collection and are extremely popular among readers. Stories such as "Nie Xiaoqian" have been adapted into movies and cartoons.

Notes Taken at the Yuewei Studio

Ji Xiaolan's collection of essays and short stories is another classic of this period. Wide-ranging in content, the collection covers such topics as customs, travelogues and anecdotes about ghosts, goblins and fox-fairies.

The Painted Skin

from *Strange Stories from a Chinese Studio*.

A scholar named Wang happened to meet a lovely girl.

Hi, miss, where are you going by yourself?

My family is poor, so my parents married me off to a rich man. The first wife scolded me every day, so I ran away.

Taken with the girl's beauty, Wang took her to stay at his home and neglected his work thereafter.

One day, Wang was stopped by a Taoist priest in the street.

You're enveloped by a thick air of evil. There must be an evil spirit near you!

Wang was frightened and went back home to see the girl. What he saw instead was a fierce ghost painting a human skin.

Then the ghost put on the painted skin and became the girl he knew.

Wang hurried to the Taoist priest, who gave him a horsetail whisk.

Hang it at your door.

He did it as the priest instructed and the girl dared not approach him.

The ghost became angry and exposed its true face.

Hmph! You won't escape from me!

The priest appeared all of a sudden and subdued the ghost.

It is because of your immoral mind that the ghost could get to you.

You may know a person's face but not his heart. A beautiful exterior may well conceal a frightening and ugly ghost!

THE DREAM OF THE RED CHAMBER

Author: Cao Xueqin (1715–1763) was born into a Manchu noble family, but his family estates were later confiscated and he was reduced to a life of poverty.

Origin: Originally titled *The Story of the Stone*, the novel comprises 120 chapters. The first 80 chapters were written by Cao Xueqin and the remaining 40 chapters by Gao E.

Content: *The Dream of the Red Chamber* narrates the decline of four great official households — the Jia Household, the Wang Household, the Shi Household and the Xue Household, with the love story of Jia Baoyu and Lin Daiyu as the central thread tying them together. As the protagonist of the novel, Jia Baoyu is often surrounded by female characters such as his sister-in-law Wang Xifeng, his cousins Tanchun, Yingchun, Baochai, Daiyu and Xiangyun, as well as a large number of maidservants, including Xiren and Jingwen. Though many, each of these characters is vividly and meticulously portrayed. Jia Baoyu falls deeply in love with Lin Daiyu, but their love faces opposition from many sides. Finally, Baoyu's family chooses Baochai rather than Daiyu for his bride. Daiyu dies of illness on the same evening Baoyu and Baochai get married. Disillusioned with worldly affairs, Jia Baoyu becomes a monk. The Jia Household falls into decline and in the end, the emperor issues an order to confiscate its estates and imprison all powerful members of the family.

Scholarship of *The Dream of the Red Chamber*: There have been many scholars devoted to the study of the novel, and over time, their work has grown into a specialised field of study. It is quite rare in world literature for a novel to be held in such high esteem.

The Story of Cao Xueqin

Cao Xueqin was born into a noble family. Later, his father was stripped of his official post and the family came down in the world.

They moved to a thatched house in the western suburbs of Beijing and were so poor that they had to live on gruel.

Cao Xueqin could not afford writing paper and had to write on the reverse sides of old books or scrap paper.

He often carried paper and a brush with him. When he got an inspiration, he would get down and write on the ground.

Look! The mad man is writing again!

Cao Xueqin spent ten years working on *The Dream of the Red Chamber* and rewrote it five times before he completed the first 80 chapters.

When Cao Xueqin was close to 49, his youngest son fell ill seriously and died because he could not afford the medical expenses. Deeply grieved, he wasted away and died on New Year's Eve that same year.

Baoyu Flings His Jade

from *The Dream of the Red Chamber.*

After her mother's death, Lin Daiyu came to stay with her grandmother, the Lady Dowager of the Jia Household. It was the first time she had met the Jia family.

Baoyu has come home!

Cousin Baoyu was born with a piece of jade in his mouth. His mother said that he dislikes studying and enjoys playing with the girls...

I have met this cousin before.

You're talking nonsense again!

Even if I haven't, she looks familiar. I feel like we're old friends meeting again after a long separation.

Cousin, do you have a piece of jade?

No, your jade is too rare for everyone to have one.

Everybody present was amazed and it was a long time before Baoyu was persuaded to put it back on.

I don't want it! All the girls here don't have one. And this new cousin is as beautiful as a fairy, yet she doesn't have one either. Clearly, it isn't a good thing at all!

At this, Baoyu took off his jade and flung it on the ground.

Daiyu Weeps Over Fallen Blossoms

from *The Dream of the Red Chamber.*

Due to a misunderstanding, Daiyu decided to pay no heed to Baoyu.

Cousin Lin must be too angry to come and sweep these withered blossoms now.

He gathered up the fallen blossoms and headed to where Daiyu and he had buried peach blossoms. He heard the sound of heartbroken weeping.

I wonder who is so unhappy and has come here to weep?

It turned out to be Daiyu, weeping as she buried the blossoms.

People laugh at me for burying fallen flowers, but who will bury me when I am gone? Spring ends and beauty fades; who will remember the flowers or the maid?

Daiyu's beauty will vanish like blossoms in the end. Baochai, Xiren and I will also end up like this one day in the future. How sad that will be!

Thinking of this, Baoyu was overcome with sorrow and cried so hard that he sank to the ground.

sob...
sob...

THE SCHOLARS

The Scholars is a satirical novel written by Wu Jingzi (1701–1754) during the Qing Dynasty. This novel strongly condemns the system of Imperial Civil Service Examination and feudal rituals. All types of scholars are depicted in the novel and Fan Jin is one of the most exemplary.

Fan Jin's Story

from *The Scholars.*

FOUR GREAT NOVELS OF EXPOSURE

During the late Qing period, there appeared several works of fiction exposing political corruption and criticising social injustices. Collectively, they are called "novels of exposure". The four great novels of this category include Li Boyuan's *Exposure of the Official World*, Wu Jianren's *Strange Events of the Last Twenty Years*, Liu E's *The Travels of Lao Can* (*Mr. Derelict*) and Zeng Pu's *A Flower in the Ocean of Sins*.

Li Boyuan's **Exposure of the Official World** pioneered the critical style in the pre-modern period. The novel was first serialized on newspaper in 1903 and was very well received by the readers.

In **Strange Events of the Last Twenty Years**, Wu Jianren portrays a hero named "The Man Who Barely Escaped Death" through whose eyes over two hundred strange events are narrated and the dark social reality in the late years of the Qing dynasty is laid bare.

The Travels of Lao Can by Liu E exposes the so-called "honest and clean officials" who also committed flagrant injustices — a topic rarely touched upon before. Written in lucid and vivid language, the novel has a more mature style and technique than *Exposure of the Official World* and *Strange Events of the Last Twenty Years*.

A Flower in the Ocean of Sins by Zeng Pu tells of the love between Jin Wenping and Fu Caiyun. The novel probes into the seamy side of society at that time and is full of patriotic spirit. The language used is elegant, and the novel is also very well-structured.

OTHER WORKS OF FICTION

Chen Chen's *The Sequel to Water Margin* narrates what happens to the heroes of the Mount Liang after their submission to the government. In the end, Li Jun hoists again the banner of uprising and goes abroad to found a nation.

Qian Cai's *The Complete Story of Yue Fei* is a full account of the life of General Yue Fei, a distinguished patriotic leader during the Southern Song Dynasty.

Chu Renhuo's *The Romance of the Sui and Tang Dynasties* focuses on the transitional period from the Sui Dynasty to the Tang Dynasty and portrays numerous heroic figures such as Qin Qiong, Luo Cheng, Shan Xiongxin and Cheng Yaojin.

Li Ruzhen's *Flowers in the Mirror* is divided into two parts. The first part describes the adventures of Old Duo, Tang Ao and Lin Zhiyang in many countries with strange customs, such as the Country of Women ruled totally by women and the Country of Little Men where double talk prevails. The author employs these strange characters and situations to expose and satirise society.

The Cases of Lord Shi, author unknown, is a group of stories on how Shi Shilun, a magistrate of Yangzhou County, handled legal cases.

Shi Yukun's *Three Heroes and Five Gallants*, first named *A Romance of Loyal and Gallant Men* and also known as *Seven Heroes and Five Gallants*, is a masterpiece describing a group of heroes and gallants who help the legendary Prefect Bao Zheng handle all sorts of legal cases.

The Gallant Maid by the Idle Man of Hebei sketches a group of loyal, filial and righteous heroes and heroines such as Thirteenth Sister, An Ji and Zhang Jinfeng to promote Confucian morality.

Shen Fu's *Six Records of a Floating Life* is a detailed autobiographical narrative of the writer and his wife written in lyrical prose.

The Country of Women

from *Flowers in the Mirror.*

Tang Ao, Lin Zhiyang and Old Duo arrived at the Country of Women. Here women dressed like men and worked outside while men wore female clothes and took care of home indoors.

How dare you pretend to be a man? Are you a hussy?

Congratulations, Madam!

Lin Zhiyang was taken by the Queen as her concubine.

Ouch! Please! I am a married man. How can I be Her Majesty's Consort?

The court maids pierced his ears and bound his feet.

It was only after Tang Ao and Old Duo promised to harness the rivers for her country that the Queen agreed to release Lin Zhiyang. The three then continued their adventures.

The Birth of Prefect Bao

from *Three Heroes and Five Gallants.*

In Hefei County of Luzhou Prefecture, south of the Yangtze River, there lived a kind-hearted man named Mr.Bao. He was known as "Warm-Hearted Bao" and had two sons — the elder, Bao Shan was faithful and honest; while the younger, Bao Hai was cunning and mean.

Madam Bao became pregnant when she was almost 50. When the child was born, Mr.Bao dreamed of a green-faced and red-haired monster with a lump of silver in his left hand and a writing brush in his right hand.

Bao Hai and his wife did not want to share the inheritance with another brother.

Ok, do it. If your mother asks, tell her the baby died minutes after birth.

Could this child be a watermelon spirit? The ancients say that a spirit in the home causes a family to come down in the world. We had better abandon it in the wilderness.

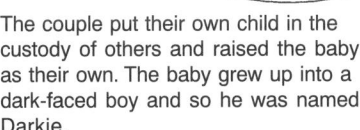

Bao Hai put the baby in a tea crate and threw it into a pit covered by long grass behind Jinping Hill. Bao Shan's wife learnt of it, and Bao Shan went and retrieved the poor baby.

The couple put their own child in the custody of others and raised the baby as their own. The baby grew up into a dark-faced boy and so he was named Darkie.

Later, the boy became the Prefect Bao. He called his brother and sister-in-law his parents and did not recognise his real parents until he was seven.

Qin Qiong Rescues Li Yuan

from *The Romance of the Sui and Tang Dynasties.*

Emperor Wen of the Sui Dynasty dreamt that he was hovering over the capital city when torrential water flooded the city as though it came down from the heavens.

This dream may foretell that someone with the radical for water in his name will endanger the country. I also saw three fruit trees. Fruit (果) is the child (子) of tree (木). Tree and child together form the surname Li (李).

All the court ministers with the surname Li became anxious. Many asked to resign and went home as civilians. Among them was Lu Yuan, who had made outstanding achievements in the northern expedition. The emperor sent him to take charge of Taiyuan.

Prince Yang Guang nursed a grudge against Li Yuan. So he dispatched a group of people who disguised themselves as bandits and planned to ambush the Li's on their way to Taiyuan.

Li Yuan was fighting a losing battle when a powerful warrior charged out and drove the bandits away.

Please stop and allow me to thank you!

The man was Qin Qiong (alias Qin Shubao), who later helped Li Yuan and Li Shimin conquer the country and found the Tang Dynasty.

You're welcome. It is only right to help when I see injustice.

DRAMA

Two prominent playwrights during the reign of Emperor Kangxi were Hong Sheng and Kong Shangren.

Hong Sheng (1645–1704)

Hong Sheng was born of noble stock. He spent over 10 years on the famous *Palace of Eternal Life*, based on Bai Juyi's 'A Song of Unending Sorrow' — the love story of Emperor Xuanzong and his beloved concubine Lady Yang.

Kong Shangren (1648–1718)

Kong Shangren was a 64th-generation descendant of Confucius. His masterpiece, *Peach Blossom Fan,* set during the fall of the Southern Ming regime, is based on the love story of Hou Fangyu and Li Xiangjun.

The Peach Blossom Fan

During the late years of the Ming Dynasty, Hou Fangyu and Li Xiangjun, a songstress on the Qinhuai River, were betrothed to each other.

After the collapse of the Ming Dynasty, Ma Ying and some others who bore a grudge against Hou Fangyu forced Li Xiangjun to marry their friend, Tian Yang.

Li preferred to die rather than submit, and committed suicide. Her blood spilled over her fan — a symbol of her engagement to Hou Fangyu.

Hou and Li's friend Yang Longyou skilfully transformed the blood stains on the fan into broken peach blossoms. That is how the name of *Peach Blossom Fan* came about.

Chen Duansheng (1751–1796)

Destiny after Rebirth is a strummed lyric written by Chen Duansheng, a talented woman writer. The lyric was once praised by the prominent scholar Chen Yinke as "First Among All Strummed Lyrics". Strummed lyrics combine speaking and singing parts. *Destiny after Rebirth* has been adapted into stories and Teochew songs, and plays based on it are also quite popular.

Destiny after Rebirth

The family of a talented girl named Meng Lijun was persecuted by some villains. She disguised herself as a boy and escaped.

She became Top Scholar and was appointed the Grand Scholar at the Hall of Peace Maintenance.

On her recommendation, Huangfu Shaohua, to whom she was engaged in childhood, was given the title of Prince on the grounds of his accomplishments.

Later, her identity was exposed. Infatuated with her beauty, the emperor wanted to take her as his concubine. Meng Lijun managed to disentangle herself by her wits.

In the end, she married Huangfu Shaohua.

POETRY AND *CI*

Wang Shizhen (1634–1711) lived during the early Qing period. He advocated romantic charms and understatement in poetry.

> **On the River**
> *Desolate and rainy, this autumn evening;*
> *Vast and broad, the Yangtze dusk in Chu.*
> *At times, a boat is seen gliding*
> *Indistinct beyond the misty river.*

Zhu Yizun (1629–1709) enjoyed a reputation equal to that of Wang Shizhen on the poetic scene of the early Qing period.

> **Tune: Bright and Lovely**
> *That year we whispered by the window,*
> *The moon bright yet not full.*
> *You looked shy,*
> *Running away*
> *Yet coming nigh abruptly.*
>
> *Unkind was the cold river,*
> *Urging us to part at the ferry.*
> *"Good-bye" was said,*
> *Wanted to leave but stayed on,*
> *Awoke with a start and tossed in bed.*

Nalan Xingde (1655–1865)

Nalan Xingde is a well-known *Ci* poet of the early Qing Dynasty. Born into a Manchu noble family, he received a good traditional Chinese education in childhood. His *Ci* poems are graceful and elegant.

Tune: Eternal Longing

Over the mountain,
Across the river,
We head for the other side of the Yu Pass,
Deep in the night, thousands of tents bright with lamps.

A gust of wind,
A spate of snow,
Breaks my heart and disturbs my dream,
No such noise heard in my hometown.

This is a *Ci* poem elaborating on homesickness.

Zheng Banqiao (1693–1765)

Zheng Banqiao was a painter and a poet. He is known for the vivid and lifelike bamboos he painted. He is one of the Yangzhou Eight Eccentrics.

Painting Bamboos in the Government Office of Wei County

Reclining in the office I hear bamboos rustling,
And wonder if it is the people voicing their pains.
Businesses handled by local officials may seem trivial,
Yet they bear directly on the livelihood of the people.

The poem calls on officials to constantly keep in mind the common folks. Even when they hear the rustle of bamboo leaves, they are expected to think of the ordinary people suffering.

The Story of Zheng Banqiao

When Zheng Banqiao served as the magistrate of Wei County, famine hit the place for several years in a row. Having nothing to eat, many common people died from hunger.

He submitted memorials asking for permission to dispense the government grain reserves to the starving people, but got no response.

Open the stores and give out the grain! I will take full responsibility.

He also spent his own salary buying food for the famine-stricken people.

Later, when his superiors held him accountable for opening the depots without authorisation, he quit his post in indignation.

When he left Wei County, he only hired three donkeys: two for himself and a footboy and the third for carrying his zither and books. Thus he bade adieu to the corrupt officialdom clean and honest.

Yuan Mei (1716–1797)

Yuan Mei was a representative poet during the mid-Qing period and he advocated writing about individual sensibilities.

> **Mosses**
> *Where the sun does not visit,*
> *Spring of itself comes.*
> *Mossy flowers, small as millet seeds,*
> *Also bloom like peonies.*

Gong Zizhen (1792–1841)

An outstanding writer of the late Qing period, Gong Zizhen addressed social and historical issues in his poetry in a critical and combative tone. This considerably enriched his poetic works.

> **Miscellanies of the Year *Ji-Hai***
> *Vitality of China comes from wind and thunder —*
> *'Tis pitiable to see thousands of steeds silenced!*
> *I'd urge the Lord of Heaven to cheer up,*
> *And bless my country with talented men.*

Tan Sitong (1863–1898)

Deeply concerned about domestic troubles and foreign invasion, poets in the late Qing period blew a revolutionary breath into their poetic works. Tan Sitong is one such poet. He felt strongly the pain of national humiliation and loss of sovereignty and was thus committed to institutional reform. He was murdered 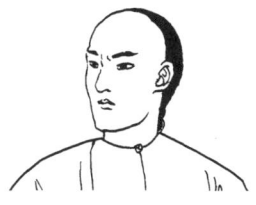 shortly after the One Hundred Days' Reform aborted. His poetry shows his sympathy for the suffering people and his concern over the destiny of China.

Tong Pass
Lofty clouds collected over this city since days of yore,
Autumn winds sent away beats of hooves.
Rivers, running through vast plains, decry their limits;
Mountains, surrounding Tong Pass, know not smoothness.

Qiu Jin (1875–1907)

Qiu Jin is a female revolutionary who styled herself the "woman warrior on a mirror lake". She liked drinking wine and was good at swordplay. Later she was captured and murdered for planning an anti-Manchu rebellion. Her poetry is filled with a heroic spirit.

Written Aboard a Ship on the Yellow Sea, When a Japanese Friend Asked Me for a Poem, and I Saw a Map of the Russo-Japanese War
Thousands of miles I travel on the wing of wind,
Alone I cross on the East China Sea as spring thunder.
I cannot bear to look at a map whose colors are altered,
When our territory is reduced to ashes in flames of war.
Unfiltered wine can never hold back tears of a patriot,
As national salvation calls for a legion of talented men.
We should pledge the blood of a hundred thousand skulls
In order to restore the universe with all our strength.

CONCLUSION

Extraordinary in its range and splendour, Chinese literature is an inexhaustible cultural treasury. Through thousands of years and dynastic changes, each age has left behind its own exceptional works and styles.

The radical sociopolitical changes resulted in a violent intellectual shock. The May 4th Movement, which took place in the political and cultural area in 1919, opposed feudalism and imperialism while at the same time promoting democracy and science. The movement also ushered in modern Chinese literature. Writers started to write in vernacular Chinese and fresh ideas were injected into their literary works. Outstanding writers came forth in great number. Among them, Lu Xun was the first to write a vernacular fictional work in modern Chinese literature — *Diary of a Madman*. He is also the author of many other influential writings such as *The True Story of Ah Q*, *Call to Arms* and *Wandering*. Other prominent writers include Shen Congwen, Bing Xin, Lao She, Xu Zhimo, Yu Dafu, Ba Jin, Cao Yu and Zhu Ziqing. Their writings are characterised by profound thoughts and a marked stamp of the time.

Whether drama, poetry, prose or fiction, since antiquity, Chinese literature has constantly evolved and enriched our lives. The atmosphere of Chinese literature in the modern age is one of great flowering. With growing cultural exchange between China and the West, Chinese literature has become an important part of world literature.

THE BIRTH OF THE MONKEY KING

Illustrated by Chang Boon Kiat.
Translated by Geraldine Goh.
150x210mm, 144 pages,
ISBN 981-229-127-X.

The irreverent Sun Wukong is the best-loved of the character in the popular Chinese literary classic, *Journey to the West*. *The Birth of the Monkey King* relates how he came into existence in the Mountain of Flowers and Fruit, and his many adventures before entering the service of Xuanzang. Be entertained by Monkey's mischief and cleverness as he fights demons and monsters from underwater and the celestial realm.

IN SEARCH OF SCRIPTURES

Illustrated by Chang Boon Kiat.
Translated by Y N Han.
150x210mm, 160 pages,
ISBN 981-229-215-2.

This is the long-awaited sequel to **The Birth of the Monkey King**. Featuring the same lovable illustrations, rib-tickling twists and a galloping plot, **In Search of Scriptures** promises to leave you breathless with exhilaration as the rebellious Sun Wukong and his fellow travellers run headlong into all sorts of adversities as they head west to gather scriptures as instructed by the Tang emperor.

ROMANCE OF THE THREE KINGDOMS VOL 1-10

This 10-volume series is a complete pictorial rendition of China's foremost historical novel *Romance of the Three Kingdoms*. The classic by Ming Dynasty writer Luo Guanzhong is based on the history of the Three Kingdoms when the states of Wei, Shu and Wu emerged from the remnants of the Han Dynasty and began to fight for power and sovereignty. It vividly depicts a series of famous battles and hundreds of historical characters in one of the most turbulent periods in China's long history.

WATER MARGIN VOL 1-6

WATER MARGIN is one of the four best-known Chinese literary classics, which also include *Journey to the West, Strange Tales of Liaozhai,* and *Dream of Red Mansions.*

Set in the Song Dynasty, the novel relates how 108 men and women gathered on Liangshan Mountain, which is today's Shandong Province in China. The heroes became leaders of an outlaw army of thousands, upholding justice and fighting against the corrupt imperial government. Historians have confirmed that the story originates from true events which took place during the tumultuous years of the Song Dynasty. Thus the oppressed masses were endeared to the account and it eventually evolved into a folk legend.

In this six-volume series, you will find a faithful account of the events leading to the assembly of the outlaws on Liangshan Mountain. Their deeds, which formed the heroic legend of a grand scale, are brought to life through the skilful hand of Singaporean cartoonist Teo Seng Hock.

中华文学之旅
先秦至晚清

编写：李小香
绘画：傅春江
翻译：杨立平

 亚太图书有限公司出版